MW01005803

"A very specific how-to-do̶ ̶ ̶ ̶ ̶
This author speaks from experience as a counseling professional, pastor, and parent. He writes as a practitioner and not simply as a theorist. *Responsive Parenting* is chock full of workable solutions for every parent who desires to be a more responsible, caring, loving, problem solving parent in a world that is advocating anything but responsibility. This will help give great insights to even the most wonderful parent. Get the book and read the book and apply the book. The results will be measurable today as well as tomorrow!"
—*Robert J. Strand, author and former pastor of 30 years*

"If you are a parent with growing children, you will want to read this insightful book. It will help you be a better parent!"
—*Dr. George Wood, former General Superintendent of Assemblies of God*

"I have known Boyd and his family for over 20 years. He is a respected missionary colleague, pastor, husband, and father. His book, *Responsive Parenting*, is a biblical and timely defense of the family at a time when this institution is intensely under attack. Each chapter is helpful to parents, grandparents, and those that might teach on the family, the raising of children, and parenting. Boyd's training and vast experience is evident in his writing, and I wholeheartedly recommend *Responsive Parenting* by this qualified counselor, pastor, and friend." —*David A. Ellis, Director Latin America Caribbean AGWM*

"We count it an honor to write a few words on behalf of Pastor Brooks and the subject matter of his book. We have known him from his teen years and have worked alongside him throughout his ministry. Boyd has always been very aggressive serving his Lord, the ministry, and his family. His work in Argentina, his pastoral leadership, and the impact of all that God has called him to perform, shows for itself in lasting results not only in lives he has ministered to but especially in his family who are all serving God today. We know each of his family personally: his wife, Marilyn, is a jewel, and his two sons and his daughter each display the fact that proper parenting is vital to a family." —*Pastor and Mrs. Charles R. Spencer, Riverdale Assembly of God, Riverdale, CA*

"A parallel idea connects the Testaments and is the promise of a time in which, by divine intervention, the heart of the parents would turn to the children and the children to the parents (Cf. Mal. 4, 6 and Lk. 1:17).

"In *Responsive Parenting*, Pastor Brooks reaffirms through Scripture and with concrete cases of his vast experience as a missionary, pastor, and counselor that these biblical truths can and should—perhaps like never before—be believed and learned. Here is a tool that equips us for the great task of being parents: a handy, easy-to-read reference manual and great text for Bible Institutes. —*Gustavo Rizzo, teacher and pastor of Centro Familiar de Adoracion, Mississauga, Canada*

Responsive Parenting

Boyd D. Brooks

Mobile, Alabama

Responsive Parenting
by Boyd D. Brooks
Copyright ©2018 Boyd D. Brooks

All rights reserved. This book is protected under the copyright laws of the United States of America. This book may not be copied or reprinted for commercial gain or profit.

Unless otherwise identified, Scripture is taken from *THE HOLY BIBLE: New International Version* ©1978 by the New York International Bible Society, used by permission of Zondervan Bible Publishers.

ISBN 978-1-58169-671-4
For Worldwide Distribution
Printed in the U.S.A.

Evergreen Press
P.O. Box 191540 • Mobile, AL 36619
www.evergreenpress.com

Contents

Acknowledgments

I want to thank my wife, Marilyn, for her incredible servant's heart. We have traveled so many places and accepted so many challenges, but none have been greater than making our marriage work and growing a family.

In the beginning of our marriage, I was a pretty lousy husband because I was so young and inexperienced. I needed help to learn how to be a better husband and father. My wife stuck it out, and together we have been blessed with three incredible children who have given us one son-in-law, two daughters-in-law, and seven grandchildren.

We are grateful to God for what we have been given. Most of all I am grateful to God for the love he has given me for my family and the passion to help others who are just starting the journey.

Introduction
Threads That Tell a Story

Jane is a thirteen year old who suffers from severe depression and out-of-control anxiety. She avoids people, feels sad most of the time, and has developed a serious eating disorder. Diana is a young mother who has lost her children to family services because of a drug addiction. Then there is Tina, a young wife who files for divorce because her husband has an addiction to video games and marijuana. Tim contemplates divorce because his wife, Susan, has had an affair. Marla is a wife and mother of three who threatens to divorce her husband because of his alcoholism. Tom and Lannie are desperate for help because they fight most everyday and have so many complaints against each other that they feel their situation is hopeless.

There is one thing all these different people have in common—a big part of what is wrong in their lives started in the home where they grew up. They were all exposed, in those tender years of childhood, to continuous unresolved conflict. There are enormous implications for every child exposed to conflict.

Responsive Parenting is a book designed to raise awareness of how important the home environment is to children's normal, healthy growth. This book is dedicated to helping parents, who are at the front lines of the parenting battle, learn to resolve conflict in the home so that their children emerge emotionally healthy. It's about parenting in such a way that your children don't have to wander around, lost in an emotional wilderness. Instead, they can enter adulthood with a sense of direction of who they are and where they are going. Is this easily done? To be completely honest, no, it's not! But can it be attained? Yes, it can—with determination and hard work. With God's help, you can transform your home into a place where conflict is resolved and the chaos is turned into meaning.

Does it really matter if a child doesn't get along well with others? The answer is an emphatic yes! The implications of a socially isolated child can be seen in countless examples of defensive behavior, ranging from a cold shoulder to a deadly shooting rampage. As more and more young people reach adulthood with no adequate model of self-regulation and conflict resolution, the more apparent this problem becomes.

Young parents wanting help are inundated with parenting materials, yet many are frustrated and left wondering about what is hindering their ability to apply this advice. Could it be that they first have to understand themselves and how they were raised before they can leave their harmful reactionary ways behind? This book seeks to illustrate the cyclical pattern of reactive parenting by helping parents first understand themselves and then understand the root cause of their problem. In addition, it will help them alleviate the problem by equipping them with the right tools to make a real difference in the way their children see and engage the world.

We are at a crisis with so many homes falling apart. The decay of marriages and the breakup of couples are leaving children exposed to very dangerous side effects. This is a wake-up call to young couples to stop the insanity of fighting because they are not only destroying their own relationship but also the future relationships of their children. When parents work on their marriage and then on their parenting skills, their family life can improve in many, tangible ways.

I have written this book on parenting not because I feel I am the most qualified, but rather because I have such a passion for the family. My wife and I have successfully raised our children and now enjoy our grandchildren, but as a family counselor, I see so many young parents struggling with the task of parenting. I know the job isn't easy, but it is worth it. My heart goes out to families who seem so overwhelmed with a variety of problems. This book flows out of the work I do with families on a daily basis.

From my perspective, parenting is more about how you handle life than anything else. How do you handle the problems that come your way? How do you handle rejection? That's important because your children will most likely respond as you do. Is anger still a problem? Do you find yourself disconnected from your parents? Do you find it difficult to resolve conflicts that arise? Your children will catch your patterns whether good or bad!

In my more than thirty years of being a pastor and a counselor, I have witnessed the impact of unresolved conflict on the family. Reactive parenting is harmful to children and has long-term negative effects on their adult behavior.

Responsive parenting, on the other hand, is what parenting was meant to be. It is the place where parents and children thrive and stay connected through meaningful communication and shared experience.

I am also a pastor who teaches the Bible to families as a guide on how to live and how to raise their families. The Bible is a relevant book full of principles that are worthy of our attention, so I have woven some biblical principles of parenting into the chapters. When understood and applied, they bring direction to our parenting.

I want to persuade parents to examine their parenting style and see which one they are using. If they are parenting from a reactive position, then I hope they will be challenged to become responsive parents. The impact on their children will be incredibly beneficial if they come to understand how important responsive parenting is.

Throughout the book I have written about several major themes that run like threads, emphasizing how important these concepts are. I have listed a few of them below. The second list describes the outcomes that are produced when you teach and live the principles:

Principles Responsive Parents Teach Their Children
- Forgiveness is God's gift to help us to manage and repair shameful mistakes in our lives.
- Self-control manages emotions like anger, frustration, rejection, and discouragement.
- Respect is honoring others—beginning with our parents and those in authority.
- Responsibility forgives, shares, helps, doesn't blame, and makes right the wrong in our actions.
- Accountability reminds us that we are answerable to someone.
- Humility means having a modest estimate of our own importance.
- Kindness is being gentle and considerate of others.
- Generosity is sharing with others in an unselfish manner.
- Industry is diligence in a pursuit or task.
- Faith is a visible relationship with God that puts him first in our lives.

Teaching the Principles That Produce These Outcomes

- Accessibility is the closeness that we feel with our parents while we are growing up.

- Clarity means making meaning out of chaos.

- Balance is dealing with both negative and positive emotion in constructive ways.

- Connection makes relationships enjoyable and meaningful.

- Acceptance is God's way of freeing us from our chains of shame.

- Authenticity is the quality of character that says I am real.

- Resolution is the hard work of resolving conflict with others in our lives.

- Modeling personifies for the child what it means to be a husband, wife, mother, or father.

- Resiliency is the ability to overcome disappointment.

These are principles that make successful families. I have woven stories from the Bible throughout because they give us examples of both dysfunctional and functional families that found grace and transformation in applying these biblical principles to their lives. I have also chosen to share experiences from counseling families over decades of ministry because some of the insights might be helpful. Finally, I have shared personal stories from my own family, not because it is such a perfect model, but rather because I know it best.

The one thing that my wife, Marilyn, and I have done that has paid off is that we have never given up. That is the definition of faithfulness, and it works. Sowing faithfully produces a harvest of blessings from God in your family.

1

Reactive Parenting: How Did We Get Here?

From my perspective as a counselor who sees many families with all kinds of problems, parenting can be divided into good and bad parenting. The good parenting I'll call *responsive parenting;* and the poor parenting, *reactive parenting*.

Reactive parenting is done in reaction to something, whether a whining child or a parent's own anxiety. It is impulsive and produces poor results. Responsive parenting is thoughtful and is in response to the child's best interests whether the child realizes it or not. Let's take a look at an actual couple from the Bible. Though they lived a long time ago, their parenting example is very relevant for families today.

Rebekah and Isaac

Reactive parenting involves a lot of games, and I don't mean fun games, but rather games of control. That's right, the players are both parents and children, and they all learn to manipulate and even use deception to get what they want. As a result, dysfunctional patterns develop and are passed on to each succeeding generation. For example, even within the pages of scripture, some of the most famous people had some very dysfunctional problems and played these games.

Jacob had a problem with deception—especially lying; interestingly, Jacob's father and grandfather had the same problem as did Jacob's children too. Let's take a look at the home in which Jacob grew up. Jacob's parents, Isaac and Rebekah, had a problem with lying, and it had a devastating effect on their sons.

Dysfunctional Patterns Cause Confusion

Isaac and Rebekah, like many couples today, couldn't have children, so they prayed about their problem. Soon the Lord heard their cry and answered their prayer. During the pregnancy the Lord spoke to Rebekah and told her that she was going to have twins and that the "the older will serve the younger" (Genesis 25:23). This troubled the couple, especially Isaac, because traditionally the oldest fared much better in regard to inheritance.

God's pronouncement over the children was not only based on his sovereignty and omniscience but also on the willingness and receptivity of each boy to follow God's heart. Isaac and Rebekah, unfortunately, never came to any understanding of how they would parent the boys, and consequently they worked against each other. No matter how badly one parent may be doing in the area of discipline, when the other disagrees in front of the children, it makes the situation much worse. This disharmony causes confusion for the children, and confusion that is never clarified causes problems later on.

Despite God's pronouncement of his will for Isaac's family, Isaac planned to give his blessing to his older son, Esau, instead of Jacob. In other words, he planned to pursue his own will and not God's will for his life and family. As he neared the end of his life and became blind, he asked Esau to prepare him the tasty venison that only Esau knew how to make. "Prepare me the kind of tasty food I like and bring it to me to eat, so that I may give you my blessing before I die" (Genesis 27:4).

It will become clear later that he never reached any understanding with Rebekah on this decision. When it comes to parenting, Isaac and Rebekah were not on the same page; in fact, they weren't even in the same book. They had both chosen their favorite child to receive the blessing and were working against each other and against their own children.

What we are looking at in Isaac and Rebekah's home is conflict. Conflict can be aggressive or passive in nature, but it always brings confusion. The message being sent to Jacob and Esau by their parents was that Mom and Dad didn't agree. Dad was going to ignore God's word to do what he wanted, and Mom was willing to deceive Dad to get her own way. When parents fail to show respect for each other or God, children are left in bewilderment, causing them to disrespect their parents, one another, and others. Essentially, how they grow up treating each other is how they will treat their future spouses.

One of the main sources of conflict that children face is marital discord. There is a clear link between children's exposure to marital conflict and children's behavioral problems. The conflict seems to predispose some children to externalize their emotions, which causes conduct problems and meltdowns.[1] One of the greatest gifts parents can give to their children is the gift of a strong marriage.

Good parenting begins with a good marriage, and bad parenting starts with a bad marriage or bad relationship for those divorced. Poor marriages contribute to poor parenting, and the result is these families live with unresolved conflict, which is so harmful to children. Strong marriages contribute to good parenting, and these families don't even have to resolve all their conflicts—they just have to sincerely *try* to resolve them. This effort proves to be a positive example to children. Let me say to those who are parenting with a divorced partner—it's not easy, but this principle will work for you too if you focus on your children and not on the hurt you may have received from your former partner.

Parenting was meant to be a cooperative effort with both the mother and father working together to provide love, security, guidance, and exemplary behavior to their children. When this happens, a child's personality and independence develop in the right way. This whole process begins at infancy and continues right on through adolescence. When a child feels secure and loved, then that child will flourish. Unfortunately, many dads and moms are unable to provide this kind of environment because of their reactive parenting style. This was precisely the case with Rebekah and Isaac.

Manipulation Is Harmful to Everyone

Rebekah reacted to Isaac's decision to bless Esau and decided to do something about it. She connived with Jacob to deceive his father and steal the promised blessing. Even though Jacob was reluctant to deceive his father, his mother convinced him it was the right thing to do. She knew even though Isaac couldn't see very well, he could still smell and taste. Rebekah prepared the venison with the same flavor of wild game that Isaac was expecting from Esau, dressed Jacob in Esau's best clothes, and covered his hands and neck with goatskins so he would appear hairy like Esau to his father.

How ridiculous Jacob must have looked with those goat skins! Only the years would tell how costly the toll of such a manipulation would be. Though their scheme seemed to have worked for the moment, they both would live to regret their actions.

Children need explanations when things don't make sense, which is why they ask so many questions. We prepare our children for adulthood by taking time to talk out their questions and help them arrive at answers that make sense. Children are put at great risk when parents use deception against each other and make this a way of life. The children are put in a bind because they begin to see that Mom and Dad don't agree and are trying to hurt each other. However, a child will understand when a parent says, "We don't agree on this issue, but we still love each other and are going to find a solution." Children just need their parents to be real.

Deception Cancels Out Authenticity

The one thing we need to give our children is authenticity. We must learn to truly be who we are to our children if they are going to be themselves. If we don't, we will effectively teach them to imitate others, thus robbing them of the strength of their own authenticity. Isaac and Rebekah did not know how to resolve their problems and come to some kind of middle ground in regard to parenting, so they dealt with their problems in dysfunctional ways. As a result, Jacob learned how to lie like a pro.

Look at how he lies to his father several times: "My father." "Yes, my son," he answered. "Who is it?" Jacob said to his father, "I am Esau your firstborn. I have done as you told me. Please sit up and eat some of my game so that you may give me your blessing" (Genesis 27:18-19).

Jacob's deception would alienate him from his father and mother and cause a rift between him and his brother. Worst of all, this pattern of deception had taken hold and would be passed on to his children. What had started as a game had now become a deadly pattern in Jacob's life. The good news is that Jacob finally did change in the latter years of his life after suffering the consequences of his actions. People can change if they get assistance by asking for God's help.

Isaac and Rebekah were reactive parents. They could not work out their differences, and they used their children against each other. Rebekah and Isaac both reacted to their boys' behavior out of anger and frustration.[2] The connection they each had with their less favorite child was a poor, emotional one charged with negative feelings. Their decisions were made in a reactive mode—impulsive decisions that were not carefully thought out.

These decisions were either too harsh or too permissive but not appropriate, and their children were left frustrated and confused. They used guilt and the withdrawal of love to coerce the children to conform to their wishes. Esau was propelled into a life of rebellion, and Jacob continued his life of deception to get what he wanted; and as a result, the entire family was separated.

Shame

One of the things that brings isolation and separates families both emotionally and physically is shame. Every member of this family experienced shame, but especially these boys, and the effects were devastating. We all experience shame in life, and many of us experience way too much of it growing up. If a child grows up in an authoritarian home, he will likely internalize his feelings and come to know the emotion of shame. Even permissive parents who are emotionally needy often shame their children by withholding their love when the child doesn't measure up. This lack of love can have the devastating effect of causing the child to begin a lifelong journey of trying to seek the approval of others. Shame can come from what others do to us or the mistakes we ourselves make. It's what we feel and what we think of ourselves that becomes so damaging.

The kind of shame I am talking about is a regretful and embarrassing event that leaves a painful memory. Brene Brown, bestselling author and researcher, defines shame as, "...the intensely painful feeling or experience of believing that we are flawed and therefore unworthy of love and belonging."[3] Little good can come from this kind of shame. Unfortunately, reactive parenting uses shame through manipulation, leaving scars that show up in adult life.

From a very early age, we need to learn to understand our emotions so we can learn how to control them. If, for example, a father tells his little son to wipe his tears away because real men don't cry—the little boy will have trouble understanding his emotions. Later, it will be very difficult for him to open up and share his feelings as an adult. A little girl who screams and kicks, to which her mother quickly responds by giving her whatever she wants so she will stop, will also not learn to control her emotions. Those experiences, characterized by unharnessed emotions, will likely bring us shame and diminish our worth, and those unharnessed emotions will sabotage our future relationships.

Authoritarian and Permissive Parenting

Two unhealthy styles of parenting from extreme opposite sides of the spectrum are the authoritarian style and the permissive style.

Authoritarian parents are notorious for creating shame in their children's lives. Because so much emphasis is put on unquestioned obedience, children grow up without the opportunity to understand confusing situations that have happened to them.

Consider Samantha who grew up in an authoritarian home where her father spoke forcefully, showed little affection, and had strict rules. His rules, such as, "No talking at the dinner table," took the fun out of life. When she broke the rules, he reacted quickly with angry words that made her feel afraid. Samantha's father threatened her, causing her to fear him. He resembled Dr. Jekyll and Mr. Hyde who had two completely different personalities. He was like a volcano on the verge of eruption. Samantha wondered how he could act like a tyrant at home and yet be kind to a stranger.

The only place she always felt completely comfortable was in the home of her aunt and uncle, so she would go there as often as she could. Unfortunately, Samantha's fears followed her into her adult years, undermining her self-confidence, and making it very difficult for her to deal with her shame.

Permissive parenting, a style of parenting that is completely opposite from the authoritarian kind, is also a form of reactive parenting that produces poor results. It too can cause confusion and shame in children as they grow up.

Loren grew up in a home with permissive parents who had few boundaries, leaving her without a sense of security. Because her father was an alcoholic, she was not able to have a close relationship with him. Although Loren never found the best role model in her mother either, she tried to find it in a neighboring family with whom she spent most of her time. Because she saw constant conflict between her mother and father, she quickly learned to avoid hostile situations by running away from them and to deal with conflict by avoiding it. Growing up with no boundaries contributed to her experiencing extremely painful and shameful encounters that happened during her adolescence. The shame followed her into adulthood and became a major adversary to leading a healthy, fulfilled life.

Although dissimilar in most aspects, these two examples have shame in common. Both children grew up under *reactive parenting*. The first child had an over-controlling parent, and the second had an under-controlling parent.[4] The over-controlling parent often causes the child to hold his emotions in, while the under-controlling parent causes the child to unreservedly act out her emotions. However, neither child knew how to identify shame in their lives, and even worse, they didn't know how to get rid of it. Because neither set of parents was emotionally available, both children found some other person with whom to connect. The authoritarian parent is not available because of the rigidity of their approach, while the permissive parent is not available because of the lack of authority and structure that shuts them out.

Reactive parenting may also use shame as the withdrawal of love to coerce the child to conform to the parents' wishes. One father realized his teenage son had left the house without permission and went looking for him. When he found him, he scolded him loudly in front of his friends to shame him. During a therapy session, I asked this parent why he had done it. He replied that he wanted the teenager to remember the incident. The adolescent certainly will remember it but not in a good way.

What every child longs for is to be loved unconditionally and accepted simply for being himself, regardless of how he measures up to external standards. When parents love the child unconditionally, the child will develop a higher self-esteem. If parents withhold their affection because they are disappointed with the child's behavior, the child will come to see himself as worthless and feel insecure. If the child is compared with another as a means of pointing out where she is failing, she will feel shame. That shame will be the cause of low self-esteem that will accompany the person throughout adulthood.

Modeling Self-Control

I have observed that children learn the dysfunctional patterns of behavior of their parents and follow them. For example, if children grow up in a home where the parents argue frequently in the presence of the children, this behavior becomes a part of their lives as adults. I can't tell you how many cases I have seen where the family was plagued by a parent whose anger was out of control. The anger problem began in their childhood and later became a pattern in their own marriage and with their own family.

Deescalating an argument and later resolving the differences that initiated the argument in the first place are learned skills. This doesn't come easily, especially if the model we grew up with was one of unresolved conflict. What helps us is to learn to ask ourselves, "What can I do to resolve this?" We need to listen and hear what our husband or wife is really saying. We need to take responsibility for our mistakes. We need to apologize and ask for forgiveness. We need to keep working on our attitudes.

It's irrelevant who started the argument—it's more important to deescalate the argument and seek a resolution. Many children have only witnessed the arguing and not the resolution. They have felt the shame of seeing one parent humiliate the other and have observed firsthand the humiliation of seeing the whole family isolated after the fight.

The remedy for shame is for parents to try to resolve the conflicts and confusion that arise, whether for themselves or for the children. Children need us to teach them the danger of not appropriately handling our emotions. They need to observe us, admit our failures, and ask forgiveness from all the family members involved. Unless we live the right way and thereby teach our children, they will follow our dysfunctional model.

Making Emotional Deposits in Our Children

We teach them the right way to handle conflict by making regular deposits of honesty and forgiveness into their lives. One day I slid my card into the ATM machine, punched in my PIN and then the rest of the numbers for the transaction. When fresh, crisp bills came out, I picked them up and placed them in my wallet. Then I reached down and grabbed my three-year-old son's hand and headed for my car. As we walked, his little mind was thinking about what he had just seen. It was the first time he had ever seen an ATM machine, and because I was in a hurry, I hadn't noticed his curiosity. By the time we reached the car and drove away, he said to me, "Daddy, you know I have some money in my piggy bank. What do you say we put our money together and buy one of those machines?" It was a great moment I have always treasured, making me smile every time I think about it. On the way home, I took the opportunity to teach my little son about the basic concept of banking, which has some real similarities to life.

If we want to make withdrawals, we have to make deposits. The only way our children will understand the significance of their lives is if we deposit the truth about who God is and who we are. Responsive parenting is about depositing the spiritual principles of God's Word in our children so that when life demands withdrawals, they have some answers. It is part of the real remedy for shame.

If you make enough deposits of love through an authentic parental model, your children will overcome any shame and develop a healthy sense of self-confidence.

2

Parenting Styles and Self-Esteem

A very important element of responsive parenting is the emotional quality of the relationship between the child and the parent. Emotional connection depends on how responsive the parent is to the child's needs and is enhanced with the use of encouragement, praise, and the showing of physical affection. Adolescents who receive parental warmth tend to engage less in disruptive and defiant behaviors and instead become involved in more positive behavior.

When adolescents feel valued, accepted, and are connected through love and respect, they don't have a problem with the parents' rules. Rules become a problem when there is no relationship. The connection between the child and the parent is the key to being a successful parent. If the child has respect for you at home and understands the value of the rules there, she will be able to do that in other places, such as adapting to the classroom and accepting the social rules at school.

When a child feels loved, he will feel special. God communicated that special love to Israel by referring to them as the *apple of his eye* (Deuteronomy 32:10). A child who is shown through the love of her parents that she is unique will develop a healthy self-esteem.

Children develop cognitive and emotional capabilities early

in life primarily due to observing the model their parents' display. If children see mom and dad treat each other with respect and kindness, they internalize those behaviors and learn to use them. Responsive parenting not only demonstrates but also helps the child understand the value of each thought or act. Responsive parenting willingly offers explanations for changing a behavior, thereby encouraging the child to respond positively. It is helpful to offer a toddler choices, but even more helpful for him to understand the value of the choices.

Staying Connected

Behavior modification that functions on a reward system effectively works for very small children, but as the children grow older, they need clear explanations from their parents. The more cooperative the co-parenting style is between the mother and father, the better the children will feel about themselves and the more respectful and adept they will be at connecting with others. They will also develop a willingness to show kindness and helpfulness toward other people. This emotional maturity will have a positive impact on their social relationships later in life.[1]

The result of a consistent, responsive parenting style, which is strong on warmth, clear communication, and self-control, seems to solve problem behavior much faster. It does it by eliminating the confusion, giving clarity, and making the child feel accepted.

When parents come to me and ask that I see their child because of a problem they are having with that child, I start with the parents not the child. Often the parents are sending mixed messages and confusing signals to the child because of an inconsistent parenting style.

Responsive parenting, while maintaining control, helps the child understand his or her emotions and helps the child interpret those emotions. For example, if a child is extremely frustrated and acting out his frustration, it is helpful for the parent to show him other ways to deal with his frustration, such as using patience and taking constructive action. Often the child needs help to break tasks down into small stages by learning to do them one step at a time. This is called scaffolding, and it is how we learn to take difficult tasks and do them step by step.

This style of parenting enhances the child's autonomy by teaching the child how to have self-control and how to be a problem solver. Children who feel accepted and connected to their parents are far more likely to embrace their parent's values and ideals. A child who grows in their ability to make good decisions will become more independent and more responsible.

Effective Transitions

Responsive parenting is parenting with a long-term view in mind. It is working to prepare your child to make the transitions from childhood to adolescence and from adolescence to adulthood. The following are several concepts that need to be communicated to children early on for an effective transition from adolescence to adulthood:

Respect for authority: Establishing this respect early will help the child be teachable.

Autonomy: The independent development of the personality and personhood of the child.

Contentment: This allows the child to develop the ability to delay self-gratification.

Conviction: A moral system that can determine right from wrong.

Perseverance: The ability to face adversity with the right attitude.

Courage: The ability to face pivotal moments in life with boldness and fortitude.

Dependency on God: The ability to trust God in difficult situations.

Patience: The ability to remain steady and wait for the results without giving in to panic.

Humility: The constraining attitude that enables a person to be authentic under pressure.

These concepts build self-esteem in the child, and they are taught through the actual experiences of daily living. As you, the parent, face the challenges that confront your family, these qualities will be on display. As the child sees them being lived out in your life, they are inspired to employ them in their own lives.

When your child feels loved and unconditionally accepted simply for being himself, regardless of how he measures up to external standards, he will have less defensive behavior. However, if your child experiences only conditional acceptance and feels compelled to measure up, he will have a fragile self-esteem that requires constant monitoring. The low self-esteem will sabotage his thinking and undermine his self-confidence.

For example, if you are disappointed with your child, you may react by withholding affection and treating him coldly. He views your actions as highlighting his worthlessness. On the other hand, if you state that you are disappointed in his behavior but affirm your love for him, he will most likely feel more secure. Every child desperately needs to know that consequences for unacceptable behavior may have to be given to him, but his behavior will never diminish your unconditional love.

Exposure to the unresolved conflict that reactive parenting causes hinders a child's normal growth patterns and increases their defensiveness. Defensiveness, coupled with low self-esteem, interferes with a child's need to interact socially. Shy children tend to internalize their problems and carry them into adolescence, causing them to experience social anxiety and depressive symptoms.[2] Hampering a child's ability to have a positive self-view and to interact with his or her peers can have devastating consequences in adolescence and adulthood. The better your child feels about herself, the better she will handle herself with her peers. If you add in the qualities of character that were just mentioned, your child will be ready to face the social challenges of life.

The Importance of Building Self-Esteem

Long-term effects of shame follow children into adulthood. Reactionary parents often have low self-esteem, and as a consequence, their reactive parenting contributes to low self-esteem in their children. For example, a child who has suffered a major loss, such as the loss of a parent through death or divorce, needs affirmation. If she is marginalized, compared, or made to feel inadequate, those feelings of deficiency will accompany her the rest of her life.

People with low self-esteem are less flexible in negative situations. Negative emotions such as anger, frustration, and resentment sap our motivation and erode our ability to cope with stress. Our inevitable response is one of having little self-control or "losing it." In addition, we find ourselves unable to improve our own mood. The thoughts that arise from our low self-esteem increase our negative emotion and fuel the perpetual cycle. Meanwhile, people with high self-esteem have a more positive self-image and have better coping strategies when dealing with negative situations.[3]

For example, a child with low self-esteem will struggle more with change, such as moving to a new school or making new friends. If parents are aware of the heightened challenges facing this child, they can bolster his confidence and give him the extra support needed to face these difficult situations. Comparing a low self-esteem child to a high self-esteem child is degrading and never helpful. A parent is never a better parent than when they accept each child as they are with their strengths and with their weaknesses. She is your child and part of you. You want that child to take away the idea that her dad and mom see her as unique—one of a kind.

People who view themselves negatively have trouble developing close relationships with others because of their fear of rejection. This fear often causes them to become self-defensive, ultimately interfering with their ability to build meaningful relationships. We can best help our children, not by micromanaging them, but by helping them acquire and develop their own social skills. They don't have to become a social butterfly, but they do need to know how to interact with people. Equipped with some basic social skills and the parent's encouragement, children will experience friendship and companionship with others, which is a self-esteem booster.

A Parenting Style That Resolves Conflict

The crucial issue is whether or not your children learn to resolve conflict. If they do, they will benefit from it their entire lives. Conflict resolution teaches children the necessary interpersonal skills that are essential in developing healthy relationships. The exposure to conflict is caught by the children and becomes a reciprocal pattern for the whole family.[4] Some children learn the dysfunctional pattern of avoiding conflict and others how to perpetuate it, but strong children learn the most essential thing about conflict—how to resolve the friction.

One of the reasons families don't resolve conflict and aren't able to transform negative emotion into positive emotion is that their words and feelings are not framed in respect. Just as a river needs banks to keep the water inside, so the family needs a respectful and constructive way of sharing negative emotion.

For example, a parent may say to a teenager, "I love you, son, and I don't want you to be offended by what I am going to say to you, but I have to be honest." That parent is framing her words in respect, which will enable the adolescent to hear and comprehend better what the parent has to say. This respectful way of speaking is necessary in every aspect of family communication. Children need to hear the truth, but they need to hear it in love. The Apostle Paul said that when we speak the truth in love, we help each other to mature (Eph. 4:15).

Negative emotion from others is difficult to tolerate, and most people don't do it very well. They usually respond with their own version as a payback to anyone being disrespectful. If we are going to put up with any amount of negative emotion, there has to be a point. If children learn early on that the point is to understand each other and work things out, they will be willing to learn how to resolve conflict.

3

Where It All Began:
Our Families of Origin

Jordan was born into a home where his father abused his mother and eventually abandoned the family. His mother survived on welfare until another man came into her life, but he brought strict rules that caused frequent conflicts.

Jordan endured verbal, emotional, and even physical abuse. He came to know the bitter shame of repeatedly being told he was worthless. His haunting memory of being paraded down the street in a headlock while his stepdad yelled out obscenities in front of his friends left him with an indelible trauma. Shameful events like that have a way a haunting a person down through the years. They are shameful memories that continually torture us unless someone helps us understand what happened and how to change that bad memory.

The way Jordan grew up also made it hard for him to love his wife and kids, not because he didn't want to, but because he didn't know how to do so. Fortunately, his wife helped him learn to love his family. For the first time in his life, he had to learn how to give and receive affection since he had never seen anyone show affection in his family.

Conflict Changes Children

There is a correlation between the frequency of loud arguments and the level of self-esteem of the child. Some children, because of exposure to conflict, may withdraw from their peers. When children are exposed to behaviors at home such as yelling, fighting, and name calling, they realize that the conflict is unresolved in their families and maybe even hopeless. In families where there is little name calling but a total avoidance of the problem, it can also suggest to children that the conflict is not resolved.[1]

Exposure to conflict puts children at a higher risk of depression, anxiety, and alcohol use. Even in homes where much of the conflict is hidden from the children, it does not spare them from the negative impact. Children feel the influence of parental conflict and are left in its wake regardless of how much they actually witness. Children exposed to conflict usually have higher levels of cortisol, which is one of the chemicals dispensed by the brain when we are under stress.[2] Higher levels of conflict are directly related to poorer psychological adjustment and impaired social functioning.[3]

Where that impaired social function is going to show up the most is when they start their own family. Adults who were raised in homes where they constantly watched their parents fight often do the same thing. They never witnessed emotional self-control in their parents, and now they find they don't possess it either. The impact of this deficit is seen in their marriages and their parenting.

Deficient Parenting

When young boys are exposed to pernicious forces, the payment will come due later in life. Those dangerous influences

21

alter rational thinking patterns and impact future marriages. Take, for example, Terrance who was given free reign from his parents to begin drinking at around age twelve. He also began experimenting with pornography early on; after all, his friends did too. When Terrance married, he discovered that his sexual temptation level was beyond his control.

Even though he was married to a beautiful woman, he still was tempted to explore other sexual avenues. The drugs and alcohol, which took an early foothold in Terrance's life, combined with his uncontrolled desire for more sexual fulfillment, caused him to be involved in inappropriate behavior. The permissive parenting style he had experienced as a child played a huge role in the destruction of Terrance's marriage, and his addictions added shame to his life.

Robert was very small when he was sexually molested by a relative. Now, twenty-five years later, he sits in my office full of resentment, having experienced shame. He was a victim of a horrible injustice in his early years, and now his marriage was rocky and unlikely to survive. Robert was the product of permissive parents who lacked structure and common sense rules in their parenting to protect their children. Children who grow up in this environment are more susceptible to entrapment because they have not learned self-restraint and discernment.

Billy was raised in a home where there was a lot of marital discord. His parents argued almost every day. Some days it got pretty bad because his dad had an uncontrollable temper, which only made the family more isolated. Billy found refuge outside of the house because he was free to go as he pleased. Billy is now in his mid-twenties, and he is struggling to make a life for himself. He never finished high school; he acquired a criminal record while in his teens and has had trouble holding a job. He still struggles with substance abuse and knows very little about handling money. Billy's life is, in part, a product of a dysfunctional and permissive parenting style. Billy is a picture of his father, and he doesn't like it.

Regina saw plenty of conflict between her mom and dad, and when she reached adolescence her dad was long gone. It was as if she had taken her father's place, and the conflict that she had long been a spectator to became her own. She left home, barely sixteen, to seek her own life. Ironically, she eventually found herself in an abusive relationship with a man just like her dad. It took several years for Regina to get the courage to leave that abusive relationship, but she finally did.

Joyce couldn't wait to leave home because she felt things would be better if she were on her own. She realized that she had messed up by getting pregnant early on, but she knew she would be happy with someone who really loved her. The problem, Joyce found out, was that finding a person who really loved her proved to be far more difficult than she ever imagined. Several marriages and relationships later she asked herself, "What went wrong?"

What went wrong with each of these examples is a family of origin that sent their children out into a cruel world very ill prepared to cope with it.

The families we grow up in influence our lives more than most of us realize. When our parents love each other and teach us how to resolve conflict, we are so blessed. When they don't, we have to learn how to do that on our own, the hard way. In our family of origin, we are either introduced to responsive parenting or reactive parenting. If it is reactive, the children will learn to react to their parents.

Children react in a variety of ways to unresolved conflict in the home. A nine-year-old boy may become very obsessive compulsive in his cleaning of the house as his way of trying to put his family back together. A teenage girl may begin to cut herself as a way of taking the focus off the family members who are fighting in an attempt to move the family into a more supportive position. Another may find some kind of escape from their family. In short, children may try to manipulate the other family members in order to make an attempt to deal with the chaos. Children will try to cope with their anxiety even if it is in a very dysfunctional way.

Substance Abuse

Parents who are substance abusers don't make good parents. Their poor parenting style translates into harsh discipline, poor monitoring, and lower levels of parental support. Their children tend to experience more aggression, rejection, neglect, low warmth, and poor interaction with them. The end result is that the child's life course and interaction with others is negatively affected. The parents' negative emotions are often internalized in the child's problem behavior.[4] Substance abuse of any kind not only takes its toll on the user but also on the children in that family.

Addictions take over people and wreak enormous havoc on their families. Parents who introduce their children to alcohol have no idea of the future impact of that decision. Their child may have all the components for an addiction, which may not show up completely until many more years have passed.

Accessibility

Reactive parenting robs children of accessibility—that very unique quality that the child feels when they are close to a parent. Children who grow up in homes where they witness unresolved conflict often experience emotional isolation.[5] A child needs to know he or she can talk about a problem with Mom or Dad any time. That accessibility is part of feeling secure and never knowing the feelings of abandonment or rejection.

Children carry with them what they learned in their family of origin, whether that is helpful or dysfunctional. If all they have known are the dysfunctional patterns of poor self-regulation with outbursts of negative emotions and avoidance behavior, they will carry on those patterns. They have learned that this is how you are supposed to do it. They may even recall the frustration and anger of their childhood but don't know how to change it. On the positive side, when they learn self-control and acquire the necessary tools of conflict resolution, things are very different. Both positive and negative styles of parenting are learned by modeling.

Children Develop the Attitudes of Their Parents

Children develop helpful attitudes and good social skills early in life primarily due to observing the model of their parents. They learn self-control if they see their parents model self-control of their emotions. Teaching children to have self-control over their emotions is the foundation for having mutually satisfying relationships in adulthood. If children see such behaviors as helping, sharing, and serving, they internalize those behaviors and use them.

Research suggests that these behaviors are acquired through

the daily exchanges of the household between the children and the parents. When a parent explains to the child the reason for changing a behavior, there is a greater chance the child will respond positively. In fact, parents foster prosocial behavior in their children when they themselves are responsive to the needs of others.

As a result, the more cooperative and co-parenting the model, the more prosocial the children will be; and likewise, the poorer the parenting model, the worse the prosocial behavior of the child. The more prosocial the children, the more likely they will have positive social relationships later in life.[6] The more exposure the child has to self-controlled parents, the more likely he or she will exhibit that same self-control.

Lifting Your Child's Perspective

Many years ago when my son Eric was very small, he was standing at my side in a very large hardware store in Argentina where we lived at the time. I had taken a number and was waiting my turn to be attended, which by the size of the line was going to be a long time. In every direction we looked, there were tools on display along with the latest building materials to gaze at while we waited. While I was busy examining the store from my view, my little son tugged on my hand and inquisitively inquired, "Dad, what does it look like from up there?" Before I picked him up, I decided to kneel down beside him and see the store from his perspective.

I have to admit that the view from above was considerably different than his view. Mostly I saw people's shoes, legs, knees, and the bottom half of a lot of things—a totally incomplete picture. Then I picked up my son and sat him on the counter where he could enjoy my view. He commented, "Things really look different from up here, Daddy." This change of perspective is helpful when parents begin to see life from their child's point of view.

Reactive parenting operates from the parent's perspective, but responsive parenting sees from both the child's perspective and the parent's. For parents to adjust their own parenting style, they need a change of perspective.

4

Responsive Parenting

There are things that require an immediate reaction in life, such as jumping out of the way of a speeding car or helping a person who is choking, but these are rare moments. Thankfully, most of us don't have to live in reactionary mode every day. We do our best work on the job when we are in a responsive mode instead of a reactive mode. We perform much better when we can make things predictable and consistent by following a schedule. So why should parenting be any different?

Reactive parenting is done in reaction to something, whether it's an obstinate child or a parent's inability to deal with their own stress. It is impulsive and causes collateral damage to those nearby. Responsive parenting requires us to be thoughtful and responsible, not impulsive and reactive. If reactive parenting is really that bad, then why do parents continue to be reactive parents? Unfortunately, parents find themselves caught in this dysfunctional style of parenting and are dealing with high levels of anxiety because this is the way they learned parenting in their childhood home.

There are also complications such as blended families. Then too, life also has a way of bringing us problems and stress to deal with. Parenting from a reactionary mode is something like a default setting, and parenting from a responsive mode is something that has to be learned.

Change Happens Slowly but Surely

Over the years in my counseling work, I have seen people with reactionary problems, such as an explosive anger problem. Repetitive habits are hard to break. Trying to undo a strong, powerful, negative pattern that has its roots in early childhood is extremely difficult for most people. A better approach is to help people concentrate their energies on building a new healthy pattern that will become stronger than the old one. The way this works is that every time the person has an episode with their anger problem, for example, they learn to take responsibility for their actions by apologizing and acknowledging what they have done. In so doing they are changing slowly and as time goes on will be less controlled by the anger.

Responsive parents have to deliberately take responsibility for irresponsible behavior in their own lives if they want to change. If you don't believe in individual responsibility, then you may not want to continue reading this book. If, however, you believe that each person is responsible for their own actions and attitudes regardless of what the circumstances are, then read on.

The parenting style that creates the best environment for children to flourish is authoritative (not authoritarian) parenting, which I call *responsive parenting*. Responsive parenting is a give-and-take style that provides children a feeling of acceptance and develops in them a healthy sense of independence.[1] It brings out their personality, applauds who they are, discovers what they are interested in, and encourages them to pursue it. The personality, skills, and interests of the child are heightened in an environment of responsive parenting.

The people who operate in this parenting style are parents who love their children and who have made a commitment to be there for each other. These parents welcome children into their home and are enthusiastic about sharing their lives with their children. They have a sense of purpose and are determined to give the best possible atmosphere to their home. Though there will be challenges and problems, they are committed to work on them together.

Responsive parenting is built on mutual respect where each member of the family is affirmed and given a unique acceptance of their differences and likenesses. Parents are committed to build each child's autonomy and self-esteem with quality interaction.[2] This interaction is authentic and brings meaning to relationships.

These parents enjoy being with their children from infancy through adolescence and are always looking forward to the moments when they are together. Children learn they can depend on their parents because they keep their word. Children raised by responsive parents learn that a promise is meant to be kept. Even when there is confusion and the child is left with questions, the parent will still be calm and bring clarity to the child's mind and spirit.

There are reasons why parents don't enjoy being around their children, such as when the children act up. Acting up is sometimes just a stage children go through. A divorce or some other traumatic event can cause children to act up or be withdrawn. Other children experience problems when one of the parents is absent for an extended period.

For some children adjusting to a new parent is very traumatic. Even though there are many reasons why a parent wouldn't always enjoy parenting, responsive parents keep working at it. They don't give up. They help their children get past the rough times, and they help turn chaos into clarity.

Collaboration Is Essential

The contributions that the mother and father together bring to the task of parenting contribute to the advantages of responsive parenting. When parents work together, their collaboration and connectedness enhance their parenting. There is no competition between Mom and Dad, just a cooperation that allows each of them to respond to the children in their own unique way. This can be tough for parents who no longer live together and especially if they don't get along too well. The responsive parent tries to find a way to make collaboration work.

Even when Mom and Dad don't live together, parents can learn to be responsive. Successful parents refuse to denigrate each other, even though there are major disagreements, because it's all for the benefit of the children. Fathers are more involved with their children when they have better relationships with their children's mother. When parents have a cooperative parenting style, they support each other and minimize conflict.

Responsive parents are problem solvers, and the children learn that Mom and Dad will not leave them alone with a problem that is bigger than they are. The result is that children learn to be problem solvers too. It's not that responsive parents rush ahead of their children, clearing away every potential problem. Instead, they empower their children with courage and self-esteem, and equip them with the tools they need to solve their own problems. Responsive parents look for opportunities to see their children grow emotionally, intellectually, and spiritually.

Staying connected when things are going well isn't difficult, but staying connected when there is some kind of conflict is another issue. For example, let's say that a little girl is dependent on her mother and is rejecting her father. Perhaps he has been out of her life for a little while. The family goes to a theme park together, but the girl wants nothing to do with her father and clings to her mother. If this father is reactive, he will resent what his daughter is doing and push her further away.

A responsive parent, however, overlooks the irritating behavior of the child and later, perhaps that evening, talks everything over with the other parent and agrees on a strategy. They talk about what is affecting their daughter and what is causing her to be fearful of being abandoned, wondering if her dad really loves her. The next day, in a context of understanding and affirmation, they talk to their daughter and affirm their love for her but also let her know that her attitude toward her dad was not right, and she needs to work on that. Because they are patient and persevering, they connect with the daughter but also teach her about her own attitude.

The responsive parenting style, while maintaining control, helps the child understand his or her emotions. This in turn builds the child's autonomy. The parents' approach to their children either enhances their autonomy or diminishes their autonomy. Those children raised in responsive homes are more likely to pursue the ideals of their parents when they are adults.[3] When parents are committed to their ideals and are consistent in pursuing them, then usually the child will embrace the same ideals.

Delayed Gratification

A permissive parent can rob their child of autonomy by not teaching and requiring discipline from their child. There are things in life that can only be learned through discipline, such as delayed gratification. Walter Mischel and Ebbe Ebbesen conducted the "Marshmallow Test" at Stanford University in 1970.

The experiment allowed researchers to view the effects of delayed gratification. Children around five years of age were offered a marshmallow. The children were told if they wanted the treat, they could have it right away; but if they waited for 15 minutes, they could have a second one. Of the 600 children who took part in the experiment, one-third deferred gratification long enough to get the second marshmallow.

Follow-up studies found a correlation between delayed gratification and higher levels of success. Those who waited for the second marshmallow later scored higher on the SAT and were generally more competent on their jobs.[4]

The responsive parent teaches their child how to delay gratification, thus teaching them how to persevere and ultimately how to be more successful. Learning to wait and be patient is a learned skill, and responsive parenting begins working on this task in the toddler stage. The permissive parent or harsh authoritarian parent does not empower the child for what he or she will face, only responsive parents can do that.

Flexible Control With Strong Leadership

Responsive parenting makes crucial contributions to the child's social development by exercising flexible control with strong, connected support for the child. It is outcome oriented for the good of the whole family.

Responsive parenting reinforces the child's autonomy and makes the child feel safe. It's easy to create co-dependent relationships with permissive or authoritarian parenting styles, but it's much harder with responsive parenting. The reason is that responsive parenting does the right thing for the good of the child even when it's hard.

Responsive parenting balances control and connectedness to

help children learn to make good choices. Here fathers and mothers play a decisive role in their adolescents' lives.[5]

Responsive parenting fosters higher levels of maturity, academic aspiration, and social competency. With less conflict in the home, along with the support of the parents, the child will want to pursue academic, social, athletic, and spiritual pursuits. Parents who provide good role models and exemplify meaningful lives inspire their children and adolescents to follow their example.[6]

The emotional quality of the interactions determines if we stay connected and includes how responsive the parent is to the child's needs along with the use of encouragement, praise, and physical affection. A warm, connected parent is associated with fewer problem behaviors in the adolescence stage. Adolescents who receive more parental warmth tend to stay focused and connected to the mutual goals that the child and parent have determined.

When adolescents feel valued, accepted and loved, they are more inclined to internalize parental values and accept parents' rules and attitudes.[7] When a child feels loved, she is strong enough to resist negative peer pressure. Adolescence can be very overwhelming in many ways for the teenager, so they need to be connected and supported by their parents more than ever. Responsive parents are aware of how connected they are to their children. When they sense something has happened to the connection, they are relentless in restoring it.

Acceptance Is the Antidote for Rejection

While visiting *Ripley's Believe It or Not* Museum in San Francisco, I had an interesting experience. You see all kinds of weird things in this place, like pictures of the skinniest and heaviest person who ever lived, the guy who swallowed knives, and the list goes on and on. Then you come to a place where you see half a dozen mirrors. Each has a face over it with a challenge for you to match that face. If you do well, red lights come on.

My family gave me the encouragement I needed, so I did my best and lit up all the lights. We then continued the tour until we came to a place where people were laughing hysterically. It took me a minute to connect the dots, and then I realized that I was looking at the other side of those crazy mirrors where people were making those funny faces. Now I was laughing at them, but a few minutes before, there were people laughing at me. I looked at my mischievous daughter who was smiling; she knew about it all along and had set me up.

This incident reminds me of something not so funny that happens to our children as they grow up in a cruel world. There is real pressure on our children to conform to the current trend, and often it is not healthy. This pressure often causes our children to try to be someone they are not. Fear of not being accepted is one of the major driving forces that our children face.

The most effective way we can prepare our sons and daughters to withstand peer pressure and overcome their fear of rejection is to raise them in an atmosphere of acceptance. In my family therapy sessions, I'm often surprised to find out that moms and dads don't compliment their children very much. What an opportunity awaits each parent to come alongside their child and build their confidence with positive parenting and encouragement!

5

Pictures of Responsive Parenting

As we have seen, the best way children learn how to become responsive parents is to grow up in a responsive home. Children learn self-control and acquire the necessary tools of conflict resolution if they are modeled. Self-control has to be learned step by step, and the best scenario is to see how parents handle conflict and stress.

The crucial issue is not whether there is conflict, but whether they learn to resolve that conflict. If you didn't grow up in a responsive parenting style, you have to learn this on your own in a different way.

Childhood Memories of Connection

Children crave meaningful moments with their mother and father. Home becomes meaningful once they experience connection. Sometimes these vital memories come from planned events, but other times they are simply spontaneous, such as going to work with Dad or having a long talk with Mom when things are not going well. It is not what the family is doing, but how they treat each other while they are sharing the experience. Randy Carlson writes these words from a book entitled *Father Memories:*

Fathers leave a lasting impression on the lives of their children. Picture fathers all around the world carving their initials into their family trees like a carving in the trunk of an oak. As time passes the impressions fathers make on their children grow deeper and wider. Depending upon how the tree grows those impressions can either be ones of harmony or ones of distortion. Some fathers skillfully carve beautiful messages of love, support, solid discipline, and acceptance into the personality core of their children. Others use words and actions that cut deeply and leave emotional scars. Time may heal the wound and dull the image but the impression can never be completely erased. Your father's best imprint upon you is best recognized of what you remember of your father's words and actions in relationship to you as a child.[1]

Whether it is with the father or the mother, these special moments create powerful, lasting memories that are essential for children. It is important to see your children as an extension of your life and not as an imposition. That makes it possible for the children to fit into your schedules so you can function as a family and not as a couple who has to entertain their children.

When children are a joy and delight to the parents, the children feel loved and accepted. Reading a story together or making a trip to the grocery store is fun. It doesn't matter what you are doing when you are doing it together. Your identity as family gives each member of the family a sense of belonging.

Both mother and father can find unique ways to connect with their children at crucial times of their lives. I routinely took my daughter out for breakfast when she was twelve, and it became a very important time in her life and mine. It was something to look forward to each week. I took my children with me on work trips and made special memories for them.

My boys helped me with projects, and I was able to teach them how to work. My wife, Marilyn, talked with all our children on a regular basis so when important decisions had to be made, she was already connected. She found a way to show our support for those special occasions that were meaningful. She made sure all their daily needs were being met and was their advocate when they needed a friend.

Establishing Authority and Discipline Early

Establishing your parental authority early on is essential to becoming a responsive parent. Every child has a tendency to disobey; they have to be taught to obey and be respectful. The time to start teaching children about your authority is in the toddler stage. If young parents begin their family with the idea that they have to give the baby everything she wants all the way through the toddler stage, they are in for a rude awakening. At some point the parents are going to want to say no to the child, and it will be a major confrontation. But why shouldn't it be, if for two years they have given in to every whim of the child and now the parents are arbitrarily trying to exert their authority.

By starting early with discipline and schedules, the child learns to cooperate, making life more enjoyable for both the child and the parents. Parents don't have to avoid events, such as going to church as a family, because they have taught the children how to behave. Granted this may not be easy, but it is certainly easier than letting the child rule the household. In the toddler stage, the parent may have to interrupt the grocery shopping and go home and deal with a temper tantrum. If, however, they do that a few times, they will be able to go anywhere they want with their child instead of dreading every public appearance.

Disciplining children begins with both parents agreeing and supporting each other. The child must learn to respect and accept the parents' authority. This is the beginning of a harmonious and fruitful relationship. If parents fail to teach the children respect for their authority, they will be handicapped from the start. Nothing is as confusing to a child as seeing and hearing his parents disagree about their approach to discipline. Whatever disagreement there is has to be worked out in private, so that you are in agreement in front of the kids.

Be Consistent

Parents, if you want your child to respect you, then you have to start teaching them to respect authority very early. Make your words mean something. If you promise a reward, make it happen. If you warn them that there will be discipline for disobedience, then give it. Be the parent and give the child an example of how to live. You have to demonstrate authority with humility for your child to appreciate and respect you.

The earlier you start with your child, the easier it is to teach respect; the later you start, the harder your challenge will be. When a child is old enough to defy you, he or she is old enough to learn the lesson of respect. Don't fall for the line that your child is different and make excuses for their behavior. In order to have a good connection with you and others, the child needs to respect you and others.

All discipline should be deliberate and thoughtful and not an impulsive reaction. The discipline should be accompanied by a clear explanation of why you are doing what you are doing. Children need to understand what's wrong with their attitude and behavior and why they are being disciplined. They also need to know that you love them, but that you will not allow that kind of behavior.

Creating an Atmosphere of Accessibility

Every child needs to be able to talk to their mother and father when they are confused. If they feel they can do this, then the parents have created an atmosphere of accessibility which will invite the child to share his or her problems with their parents. This availability is really your attitude toward your children. If they are your number one priority and a source of pride, then they will sense they have an open invitation to come to you. The older they get, they will continue to come to you when they need help.

The child wants to know deep down that Mom and Dad will be there for him. The gift of making yourself available to your children will empower them to succeed. Some parents don't realize that because of their reactive mode and overload of stress, the message they are sending to the child is, "I'm too busy to hear you." Accessibility is something the child actually feels and accepts. Responsive parenting creates this kind of atmosphere and removes any fear of coming to you.

Resolving Conflict Through Forgiveness

Learning to forgive is essential to responsive parenting. We have to comprehend that resentment fuels conflict in a relationship and impedes resolution. To the contrary, forgiveness offers an escape door from the boxed-in position that the conflict imposes on us. We are never trapped in a resentment and hate cycle when we forgive.

Forgiveness opens the door that hate imposes on us and invites us to come out. Forgiveness interrupts the toxic pattern and gives people an exit strategy from the negative cycle.[2] Many parents are caught in a cycle of resentment of a former spouse, and the negative attitude becomes part of their parenting. Forgiveness is the most effective method of changing this. You can't teach your child how to forgive if you still have people in your life you haven't forgiven. The Lord's Prayer teaches us to forgive on a daily basis: "Forgive us our sins, for we also forgive everyone who sins against us" (Luke 11:4).

Mom and Dad have to learn to forgive each other if they want to teach their children how to forgive. Forgiveness helps parents regain a more balanced and compassionate view of the offender, empowering them to give up the right to seek revenge. Grudge holding and spiteful treatment of the other person weaken the bond between parents and prohibit them from working as a team. When a parent has lingering anger about a betrayal or deep hurt, then that parent often harbors a desire to punish his or her partner. As a result, these attitudes weaken the parenting alliance and expose the children to parental conflict.[3]

Jacob was a grudge-holder until he learned to forgive. God changed his name from Jacob, which means deceiver, to Israel, which means God-contented. That is the kind of change we need to introduce to our children because it frees them from our grudges, resentment, and prejudices.

Forgiveness is God's gift to keep our lives free of clutter, like a giant shredder that grinds up all the junk in our lives and sorts it out. If not for forgiveness, we would accumulate much hurt, resentment, bitterness, and even hate. All these powerful negative feelings can follow us through the years and cut us off from people who have hurt us. As parents, we pass our hurts and resentments on to our children. However, when we choose for-giveness to be an active part of our lives, we consistently deal with the hurts as they come to us. Since our children are always watching us, they too will learn a healthy practice of forgiveness that will accompany them into their adult life.

Have you ever noticed that so many stories glorify the person who takes revenge—the one who gets his pound of flesh? That's the way we are wired—we want people to get what's coming to them. Jesus came to teach us another way to live. He taught us that greatness is not found in taking revenge but in forgiving. Forgiveness is God's gift to us.

Responsive parenting introduces children early to forgive-ness. It shows them what it means to forgive and how to act to-ward someone you have forgiven. Forgiveness is a deliberate choice. You have to choose to be a forgiving person. When we forgive each other in our families, we give the gift of forgiveness to our children. Forgiveness is truly a gift to be shared, but it takes practice to learn how to share this gift.

When our children were very small, I remember how diffi-cult it was for me to accept the idea of forgiveness on a practical level. It goes both ways: we forgive, and we ask to be forgiven. Our family was having breakfast when my toddler son spilled his milk. I reacted by scolding him, and he immediately started crying. I went to the kitchen to get him some more milk and in the process spilled a whole lot more milk than he did. I hate to admit it, but my first thought was to quietly clean it up and not say anything, but I knew that wouldn't be right. As hard as it was, I returned with the milk and apologized to my son and the family. That act of forgiveness healed my son's little heart and taught me this is the only way I would be able to teach my family about forgiveness. I would have to be the first to ask for forgiveness when I did wrong, which would be more often than I would like to admit.

Apologizing to people is one of the ways we open the door to forgiveness. No matter what it takes, we have to forgive, even those who won't forgive us. It is so much easier to make excuses, but the truth is we have to accept the consequences for our actions and make things right between us and the person we wronged. True forgiveness requires that we make apologies for any wrongs or actions on our part. We articulate what we did without making any excuses and apologize. True apologies invoke forgiveness.

The benefits of forgiveness are wonderful, but the consequences of not forgiving are devastating. I sometimes say that "It only takes one to save a marriage," meaning it only takes one to stop an argument and bring healing by apologizing. How many marriages could have been saved from divorce if even one of the spouses had learned to say these simple words, "I'm sorry." Dick Keys writes insightfully about our difficulty of offering apologies:

> Apologies are never easy, but apologies for resentment are among the most difficult. This is because the same pride that drives us into resentment, blocks our retreat from it. Think of the difference between the ways a squirrel and a cat climb a tree. The squirrel has the equivalent of your thumb on the back of its front paws which enables it to scamper down a tree as easily and neatly as it goes up it. The cat, on the other hand, has only claws on the front of its paws. It can climb up a tree very nicely, but it is a great indignity for a cat to come down. It must come down backwards, usually very slowly, twisting and clutching at

the bark, looking over one shoulder. A cat might climb to the top of a tree and the fire department comes to carry it down on a ladder. In our rush into anger at high speed and with great ease and there we sit in the high branches, with the reminder, "Anger lodges in the bosom of fools" (Eccl. 7-9). To get rid of resentment can be an awkward and humiliating experience. Like the cat, we too would rather wait until someone hears our howling and sympathizes with us, and helps to carry us down from our perch with gentleness and dignity. In short, we wait for the other person to apologize to us.[4]

Getting past the hurts others have done to us is vital to enjoying our future. Unless we are able to forgive and allow God's forgiveness to heal our broken hearts, we will never see the future God has for us. One time when ordering Chinese food, I received a fortune cookie that read: "Time heals all wounds." How often we have heard this refrain, but it is simply not true. Time alone is not enough to heal our deepest wounds; only God can do that through the gift of forgiveness.

Life Is About More Than Just Me

Viktor Frankl was a psychiatrist, Auschwitz survivor, and author of *Man's Search for Meaning*, which has sold over 12 million copies worldwide. When he was asked about his book, he responded with a unique answer. Here is the exchange:

"Dr. Frankl, your book has become a true bestseller—how do you feel about such a success?"

He responded, "I do not at all see in the bestseller status of my book an achievement and accomplishment on my part but rather an expression of the misery of our time: if hundreds of thousands of people reach out for a book whose very title promises to deal with the question of a meaning to life, it must be a question that burns under their fingernails."

Only humility would prepare a man to give such an answer. It is not surprising that Dr. Frankl responded the way he did because he had a proper view of himself and life around him. In the Nazi concentration camps, he refused to hate those who treated him so badly. Even though they took from him everything he owned, he was determined to retain his ability to forgive, and that kept him alive. And later in life, it was this same worldview that kept him free from the power of success to taint him.[5]

Viktor Frankl saw life as bigger than himself. He saw meaning in serving and helping others. Responsive parenting teaches this kind of a world view early on. We must help our children find meaning in life apart from and beyond seeking their own happiness.

A wonderful example of this is the story of Queen Esther in the Bible. She is a gracious and courageous woman who saved her people from complete annihilation. How did Esther get that courage and fortitude to be the brave young woman she was? She got it from her older cousin and father figure, Mordecai.

He planted the seeds of affirmation, along with a proper fear of God in her. Mordecai modeled integrity for his "daughter." Consequently, she saw godly character lived in the daily routine of life, and Mordecai's values became her values. She chose to live the life modeled by her family. She respected and admired her "father."

In the same way, our children's response to the truth of God's Word is primarily dependent on how well they see it modeled in our lives (although they still have free will and make their own choices). Children by and large emulate what they see in their mother and father. God's plan for each of our lives is to imitate Christ. However, Christ-like purpose has to be learned through a model. If they see a life in their parents that is bigger and better than a personal pursuit of happiness, they will be likely to embrace it.

Contentment Is a Gift

Contented people are rare; that's why they make such an impression on us. They draw their contentment in life from God, not from their circumstances or the people around them. Contented people don't spend time wishing they were someone else or that they could be some other place. We don't meet them too often, but when we do, we don't soon forget them. Especially in today's society, children are learning they must have what they want when they want it mainly because their parents are living in the same way before them.

We give our children such a huge advantage when we teach them how to be content with what they have. Chances are they won't emerge under a mountain of debt as they begin their adult lives. They will probably have much more free time because they won't be enslaved to pay for things they really don't need. They will place a higher priority on people than on things. Contentment is a discipline that helps us learn what is important in life, and first on that list is people.

My wife, Marilyn, usually had more insight than I did into what was going on in each of our children's lives as they were growing up. Sometimes she could see the problem, and sometimes she could only detect the symptoms. In either case, we nurtured contentment in our children and pulled out any weeds of discontentment that sprouted. We taught them they were privileged by enumerating the many ways in which they were blessed. We were hard as steel on self-pity and relentless on greed, but we affirmed their strengths and applauded their accomplishments. We both knew that our children would only learn contentment if we taught it to them, so that meant constantly working on our own attitudes.

Personality Development

One of our primary tasks as parents is to help our children discover their purpose in life. In so doing we help each child find their reason for living. Solomon said, "Train a child in the way he should go, and when he is old he will not turn from it" (Proverbs 22:6). It is discovering *the way* she should go that I'm referring to. This *way* is a special design that God gave each child, and we must ascertain what that way is, and then parent them in that unique way.

The wise man Solomon also gave us some good advice when he said, "Even a child is known by his actions, by whether his conduct is pure and right" (Proverbs 20:11). Observing our children will help us see clues to understanding the God-given purpose in each of them.

The key is to learn who they are, so we can help them learn what they are to become. Are they artistic or athletic? Maybe pensive or talkative, analytical or impulsive? Each is a clue to help them find something worth living for. It is exciting for young parents to watch the young toddler show a bent or curiosity for a certain area such as music, science, or art. Then we slowly and deliberately help facilitate that uniqueness so that it grows. Often times children who grow up without this kind of parenting flounder for many years of their early life. Later in life they regret the wasted years.

If we see musical ability, artistic design, or mechanic inclination, we facilitate that and watch this interest grow. Our acceptance of their personality and inclinations means the difference between their pursuing them or being ashamed of them. Recognizing their personality very early in infancy and in the toddler stage is something to rejoice about. Personality development is enhanced when we recognize that this is a one-of-a-kind person emerging. We, however, must trim and cultivate the plant while letting it bloom.

We also enhance the development of our children's personalities when we help our children to be more socially adept. Helping them learn to get along with their siblings and playmates is preparing them for better things to come. During their early years, we observe them and keep a keen eye on their interests and passions.

The Sharing of Values Creates Cohesion

One of the most important things we do as parents is sharing our values and beliefs. If we have learned what is meaningful for us in life, then we share it, and our child accepts it early on. What they look for as they get older is whether the values are consistently lived out in our lives. If they are, then the values will be fully embraced in their adult life, and if they are not, they will probably be rejected.

Cohesion is where the rubber meets the road and where people really find a way to live out their beliefs in resolving conflicts. Research suggests that when a family has cohesion, conflict is moderated and resolution is more common.

Consequently, the children, despite conflict, feel loved and cared for. There is a strong correlation between the quality of parenting and the transmission of values and ideas to children. The quality of parenting has an impact on whether the children raised in the home will appropriate the religious and spiritual beliefs and practices of the parents.[6]

Cohesion is what we have in common and what we share with each other. If, for example, the principle of responsibility is lived out clearly and explained, then your children will share this common value and later share it with their children. If, on the other hand, there were gross inconsistencies in what you, the parent, said and did, the values will most likely be rejected.

6

Responsive Parenting Strategies

Parenting can be exciting, but we have to have our priorities right beginning with the marriage. If the marriage is strong, then parenting is much easier, and the family enjoys life together and solves its own problems. Sadly, today parents often live their own separate lives, and each of the children live their own lives apart from the other family members. Consequently, they share few meaningful experiences together.

Eating meals together is the perfect place to talk, laugh, and support each other. Working together provides the opportunity to teach children about responsibility. Playing together and having fun is what family time is all about. Going to church and worshiping together provides the opportunity to understand and share your faith with your children.

Decisions to involve the children in activities should be based on what's best for the family and on what interests the parents and children have determined will be beneficial for each child. These kinds of decisions should be made thoughtfully so that once a child becomes part of an activity, they learn to make a commitment to it. Parenting is not about keeping your children from being bored as much as it is about teaching them how to live life.

How Parents Treat Each Other Impacts the Children

When parents argue, they often exaggerate each other's faults because they are upset. The offended parent then digs their heels in and refuses to acknowledge any wrong, and the argument becomes a fight. It is hard to be a responsive parent when you are angry at your spouse. Responsive parenting means the parents exercise self-control in their lives, and the children learn from them.

When one parent treats the other with condescension as if he were speaking to a child—the children learn the wrong way to treat their mother or father. Anger travels with disrespect, and they always leave hurt and rejection behind. When children see their mother shows respect to their father and their father loves and respects their mother, they imbibe those feelings. They not only learn how to treat each other in the family, but also how to treat their future wife or husband.

Just like the announcement on the airplane about how it is important to put your oxygen mask on first before putting on your child's, it is essential to first and foremost concentrate on being a good wife or husband and then a good father or mother. Nothing could be more ludicrous than to conceive a child so that the marriage will get better. If you put your children before your marriage, you will be putting the cart before the horse.

Husbands and wives have to work at staying connected. They have to overcome any interruptions to their emotional connection. When the door seems closed, don't try to kick it down, rather patiently wait for it to open. It will open if you are there to see it. Husbands and wives need to connect emotionally several times each week. It might be for a few moments or for an entire day. It might be through leisure or while talking through a difficult situation, but they are connecting. Connecting is what keeps your family together and safe from outside intrusions. If you are emotionally connected, you will be strong enough to deal with the emotional demands of parenting.

Acceptance Enables Children to Overcome Obstacles

What changes everything in marriage and the home is acceptance. Acceptance of everyone with all their warts—just like they are—brings people together.

We assume the attitude of helplessness when we think that life is not going to get any better and nothing we do will ever change it. Change is not easy and takes courage and patience, but we can always make things better if we are willing to try.

I have underscored the importance of acceptance because it is crucial to parenting and connecting with your children. When acceptance is an essential part of your family, children can be resilient enough to overcome even the parents' shortcomings. If the parents are willing to admit their shortcomings and apologize, children are more than willing to forgive and will demonstrate a resilient spirit.

Being willing to listen to our children and know how to respond is imperative. Accepting our children is half the challenge; the other half is teaching them how to live. We ultimately have to teach them how to behave in all situations, which means we have to discipline them. They also need explanations of how to behave and what is and isn't acceptable behavior. Those explanations work best if given in moments of love and acceptance coupled with consistent discipline. Our children need to know their mom or dad really mean what they say.

Our discipline, however, should be tailored to the child. Dr. James Dobson shared this story in his book *Bringing Up Boys:*

> *Smithsonian Magazine* once featured a master stone carver from England named Simon Verrity, who honed his craft by restoring thirteenth century cathedrals in Great Britain. As the authors watched him work, they noticed something very interesting. They wrote, "Verrity listens closely to hear the song of the stone under his careful blows. A solid strike and all is well. A higher-pitched ping and it could mean trouble. A chunk of rock could break off. He constantly adjusts the angle of the chisel and the force of the mallet to the pitch, pausing frequently to run his hand over the freshly carved surface."[1]

The story demonstrates God's love and patience with us as he constantly works to bring out his plans in our lives. This is what Paul wrote in his letter to the Romans: "And we know that in all things God works for the good of those who love him, who have been called according to his purpose" (Rom. 8:28).

This story also eloquently describes the task of a sensitive parent who is well connected to the child. He or she knows when to let up and when to bear down because they listen. It takes patience and a watchful eye to discipline your child the right way.

Change—Be Flexible and Not Rigid

Old patterns are difficult to overcome and can make change appear unattainable. Most of us find change difficult if not practically impossible. The way to overcome bad habits is to institute a new habit, and as the new habit becomes a new pattern, it will overtake the old. If bad habits are interfering with your parenting, identify them and begin to work together with your spouse on them. For example, one parent may have the habit of giving in to a whining child instead of being consistent with the agreed upon strategy. Another parent may have the habit of ignoring the kids by zoning out. Admit the tendency and together work out a new approach that will replace the old habits.

Learning to be flexible is invaluable as a spouse and parent. Life rarely goes according to plan, and if we maintain rigid expectations of those around us, we will experience intense negative emotions, and so will they. We often grow up with a mentality of expecting people to treat us a certain way or to do things our way. When they don't, we experience anxiety and allow our emotions to be controlled. If, on the other hand, we can adjust our expectations to the changing circumstances, we will be able to maintain better self-regulation, which can make a big difference in a growing family. Inflexibility will produce anxiety in our children, and our rigidity will be picked up by them. A flexible approach to the unexpected, on the other hand, will minimize conflict and teach the children how to roll with the punches.

Learning how to recognize situations that require some variation is the first step in learning how to be flexible. It's important to examine one's expectations and look for rigid and unrealistic expectations that are going to set us up to fail. Learning the value of being flexible is important because it helps us preserve the peace and enjoyment of the moment for both persons.

Many years ago while living in Argentina, I flew to another city and took a taxi to a friend's house with whom I would be staying. They weren't home, so I sat outside along the fence waiting for them and watching some little children across the street play games. They were having a ball when suddenly a pickup truck screeched to a halt by their house, raising a cloud of dust. It was their father whom they eagerly greeted with "Hola, Papi."

Despite the excitement of his little children to see him, the father never returned their greetings. Instead, he yelled at them to get out of his way while he raced toward the front door, kicking toys out of his path. He entered the house and immediately started yelling at his wife. In a few minutes he raced back outside, got back into the pickup, and sped off. The quiet, fun-loving house had been transformed in a matter of minutes into a home filled with anxiety, sadness, confusion, and anger. There were cries and sobs coming from both inside and outside of the house—all because of actions of a careless father. I watched the dust settle as the cloud his pickup had stirred up from the dirt road slowly drifted down.

I couldn't help but wonder what life would be like for this man in 20 or 30 years after the dust of his influence had really settled. Would there be any regrets of how he treated his family? I imagined there would be plenty. If this is the way he treated his family on a day-to-day basis, I wondered how his children would treat him in his old age. I don't think our greatest regrets in life will come from not having done greater things at work or not having experienced greater leisure. I think it will come from not connecting with our families and not enjoying them more. No one regrets not having mown their lawn more, but they do regret not having connected with their family more often.

We all face situations that give us anxiety, but mature parents are able to adapt their attitudes, make allowances, and not take out their irritations on their children. So many of the things that are so upsetting today won't even exist tomorrow.

Cultivate Maturity and Common Sense

Arguments between a husband and wife are often over silly things that don't matter that much. They do matter, however, in the scheme of your ability to make your marriage work and be a responsible parent.

Imagine a couple coming home and seeing smoke spewing out of their house. Instead of jumping out of the car and putting out the fire or calling 911 immediately, they begin arguing over who started the fire. He blames her for leaving the stove on, and she blames him for not turning off all the lights. Now the smoke is thick and flames are escaping out the window, but still they remain locked in an intense argument as to who caused the fire.

No sane person would do that! Instead, a normal response would be that you would jump out of the car and put the fire out if you could; and if you couldn't, you would call the fire department immediately to save your house. But people react inappropriately all the time in regard to their marriage.

When couples argue incessantly, it doesn't matter who started it—what matters is who can resolve it. It takes maturity and common sense to take responsibility for your actions and work on creating harmony instead of conflict. Sometimes it means getting counseling or reading a book together. You need to do whatever it takes to cultivate maturity in your marriage and family.

Forgiveness Is a Wonderful Gift

Forgiveness is God's answer to our sin, and it is the lubricant that keeps our relationships working. However, have you ever noticed that many Christians still deal with a sense of shame long after they have been forgiven? Hurtful memories of shame experienced in their earlier years still haunt them. Shame is one of the most powerful negative emotions a human being can experience, and it leaves a scar that is a constant reminder of that dreadful experience.

God's answer to our shame is his unconditional acceptance of us. Most people have never known unconditional acceptance. The acceptance they have known has always been predicated on performance. Many have been raised in homes where they were compared with others; when they didn't meet their parents' expectations, they experienced shame. Some people carry deep scars from the shaming experiences received at the hands of bullies or even neglectful or uncaring teachers. Others have worked in environments where they have been publically shamed for not achieving their boss' expectations.

God wraps his arms around us and tells us that we are accepted, and that acceptance eradicates our shame. This is beautifully illustrated in the parable of the Prodigal Son in the gospel of Luke. When the younger son rebelled against his father and asked for his inheritance even before his father's death, the father surprisingly complied with his request. Upon receiving his portion, the son traveled far away only to waste his money. His life spiraled out of control until he hit bottom.

> *While feeding pigs he "came to his senses," and said to himself, "how many of my father's hired men have food to spare, and here I am starving to death! I will set out and go back to my father and say to him: Father, I have sinned against heaven and against you. I am no longer worthy to be called your son; make me like one of your hired men." So he got up and went to his father* (Luke 15:17-20).

Most likely this son had been gone for years, and though the father had never gone looking for the son, he never gave up hope that he would return. Luke beautifully describes the scene,

But while he was still a long way off, his father saw him and was filled with compassion for him; he ran to his son, threw his arms around him and kissed him (Luke 15:20).

The picture of the father running to the son, throwing his arms around him, and kissing him is one of acceptance. I love that scene so much! The son gave the following speech that he had rehearsed at the pig pen,

"Father, I have sinned against heaven and against you. I am no longer worthy to be called your son." However, he did not give the whole speech because the father interrupted him with this response of acceptance, But the father said to his servants, "Quick! Bring the best robe and put it on him. Put a ring on his finger and sandals on his feet. Bring the fattened calf and kill it. Let's have a feast and celebrate. For this son of mine was dead and is alive again; he was lost and is found." So they began to celebrate (Luke 15:21-25).

This is a picture of how God responds to all sinners who return home. We long for acceptance, and in the Father we have it. The shame of our past and the scars we carry are covered by his acceptance. Even though we don't deserve to be a son or daughter, the Father receives us as such and accepts us into the family.

I don't know anyone who doesn't have a bad memory or two, but some people seem to have too many to count. Those bad memories have contributed to dysfunctional patterns of thinking. These people have been hurt so severely that they have tunnel vision. They see most everything as a loss instead of a gain. They focus on the problems and not the solutions.

When my father was just a small boy living in West Texas, he attended a one-room school house when he was in the fifth grade. His education was intermittent, leaving him with gaps in his learning. When he failed to solve a math problem one day, the teacher ridiculed him in front of the other students.

He never forgot that experience, and the feeling of his inadequacy, especially when it came to math, seemed to grow. His formal education ended that year. Later on, during World War II he was selected for officer's training and, according to his captain, would have made a fine officer. However, when the training required some math, my father walked out of the class and left the program. He carried too many terrifying memories of a fifth grader who couldn't do math.

Changing the Way We Look at the Past

I have learned that the best thing any of us can do with bad memories is to invite Jesus into that memory. Jesus is not subject to time. He is eternal, and he can travel through time. He will stand with us in remembering that moment when we first stood all alone. He will stand with us in recalling that moment when we were filled with disappointment and sadness.

When we felt stupid, useless, and inadequate, he comes to change those feelings of loss. These are wounds that never heal and memories that never go away on their own. The enemy uses them to taunt us all through our adult life. When we invite Jesus into the memory, he comes to correct the lies and defend us from the slander. He comes to set us free from those enslaving memories.

This is what the Apostle Paul meant when he said, "The

weapons we fight with are not the weapons of the world. On the contrary, they have divine power to demolish strongholds" (2 Cor. 10:4). To parent in a responsible way, we have to let God heal our shame and make us strong. Then we will be able to help our children face their shame.

Seizing the Special Moments

When my son Ryan was just a little guy, he had a favorite blanket that was worn to shreds. My wife washed it with care because it was so frayed on the edges. We tried to give him a new one, but he only loved the old one.

On a trip from our home in Argentina to Brazil, we spent the night in a hotel. The next morning we had breakfast and continued our journey. We drove for several hours and then discovered his special blanket was missing. In an effort to console our distraught little son, I promised to stop at the hotel on the way back and ask about the blanket. That promise really seemed to calm him down.

In reality, I didn't think there would be much hope of finding the beloved blanket. If anyone saw it, they wouldn't think twice about tossing the worn-out thing in the trash. On our return to Argentina, Ryan asked often about his blanket. When we finally arrived back at the hotel where he had left it, I inquired if anyone had found a little boy's blanket. The manager said, "Just a minute," and returned with the blanket. He informed me that a maid had brought it to him and told him it had great value to someone—so he put it in the safe and waited to see if the owner would return.

I have never forgotten how excited and comforted our little boy was to recover his blanket. Though he was still little, he was experiencing anxiety; however, it helped him to know that we all understood and were concerned about what he was feeling.

There isn't a person on this planet that doesn't need that same experience of knowing someone cares. We all want someone to validate our feelings with words like: "I know what you are going through" or "I feel for you right now." It does something for us. Every child needs for her parents to validate her feelings. Every husband and wife needs their spouse to validate their emotions.

We never met the kind maid in the city of Posadas, Argentina, who safeguarded Ryan's blanket because she recognized it was valuable, but I am grateful for people like that. She had a quality that all of us need as parents—the ability to see value in things that others would overlook. That kind of awareness will help our children overcome their anxious and shaming experiences.

7

Helping Our Children Grow Their Personalities

When a child is loved and feels safe, the brain is free to develop, which means the child's personality is going to develop the way it should. When a child feels safe, their physiological and psychological growth gets a green light from the brain, enabling remarkable growth.

We all experience a heightened fear or tension when we sense a threat, which is a normal response to perceived danger. Responsive parents find ways to pull out all the stops, creating an environment where children flourish physically, psychologically, emotionally, cognitively, socially, and spiritually.

Whenever parents use arbitrary and authoritarian approaches to parenting, the children will react, and often those reactions are not positive. Reactive parenting is unwilling to hear the child's protest or complaints with explanations. Because many busy parents spend very little time with their children during the week, they often lack the physical energy to engage children until the weekend. Staying connected and engaged, however, is the greatest antidote against low self-esteem and is the best way to parent children.

Children who grow up not liking themselves have greater difficulty making friends because of their concerns about rejection. These concerns often trigger self-defensive behaviors that interfere with building meaningful relationships. Furthermore, individuals with low self-esteem sniff out minor threats in others' body language or conversation, thus activating a defensive reaction in the brain. As a result, these same individuals are more likely to feel rejection.[1]

Rejection is one of the most difficult human emotions to deal with. If a child learns how to deal with it early on, they will be miles ahead in preparing for future feelings of rejection. If they don't, they will be overwhelmed with feelings of inferiority throughout life.

Biological Response to Threatening Stimuli

Research about the brain reports that in order for children to create relationships, they first must subdue their defensive reactions. Researchers have identified the areas of the brain where detection and evaluations of features take place, such as body and facial movements.

In the presence of people who are safe, children undergo active inhibitions of the brain areas that control defense strategies, enabling them to engage spontaneously in social interaction.[2] When we sense there is a threat, the brain releases chemicals to equip us to respond to the threat. When the threat has passed, the body has a built-in system for shutting down the threat response. Herein lies part of the problem with many children. That turn-off button does not always work effectively in the presence of on-going tension and conflict, so they remain hyperactive. This is one of the reasons we see so many children on medication for attention deficit disorders.

Two negative extremes exist in families that hinder balanced growth in children. Some families tend to over-control their children by keeping them under tight control too long, which definitely hinders their self-autonomy development. They have not parented in such a way as to prepare the children for an eventual healthy departure. Then there are other families that tend to under-control their children, sending them out on their own way too early.

Both extremes leave adolescents, who are emerging into adulthood, vulnerable to emotional instability and unprepared to meet adult challenges.[3] Most of us parents want to see our children succeed, but we have to help our children seize the opportunities that come to them. Childhood and adolescence are times when parents can equip their children with the right tools for success by helping their personality and gifts grow.

Helpful Strategies for Defensive Behavior

The following are some of the factors that contribute to responsive parenting: autonomy, acceptance, forgiveness, resourcefulness, and emotion regulation.

1. Autonomy. First, people with higher autonomy generally develop a higher threshold at which they feel compelled to self-protect when facing a threat. In other words, if you help your children have a higher self-esteem and equip them with the vital tools for life, they will be more comfortable in their own skin. They will be less judgmental and critical of others who are different and less opinionated.

With responsive parenting, children learn that there is nothing wrong with having strong opinions as long as we are willing to hold those opinions until the right moment.[4] Autonomy is also the child's ability to function on their own without a dependency on the parent. Developing this autonomy and independence will strengthen their self-esteem and sharpen their social skills. Autonomy is the foundation on which adult life will be built.

2. Acceptance. Conflict offers not only the threat of alienation but also the possibility of intimacy. One of the best things parents can teach their children is to not be afraid of negative emotion in other people. Just because someone is angry or upset, they don't have to get that same way. They can learn to remain calm and try to understand what it is that has made the person upset.

Parents can break the negative spiral of immediate reactive behavior through acceptance of the difficult child, thus teaching that child to do the same. When acceptance comes first, it opens up the way for change by enabling a parent to accommodate the needs of each child.[5] When parents and child overcome a conflict with a sense of resolution and understanding, they become more connected.

When parents see their child struggling, whether in childhood or adolescence, it is an opportunity to better understand the child. These moments are crucial for each family and can be blessings that bring the family closer together if they truly seek resolution. These conflicts actually offer the opportunity of greater intimacy.

3. Forgiveness. God knows how imperfect we are, so he gave us the gift of forgiveness. Family members who have learned to forgive show more grace to each other and stay more connected. Those who don't forgive are more resentful and more disconnected. Children best learn forgiveness by watching their mother and father demonstrate it.

4. Resourcefulness. Effective parenting requires resourcefulness because defusing conflict can be as hazardous as defusing a bomb. Humor can be an effective strategy for regulating stress and defusing negative emotions. Children need help to learn how to laugh at their own mistakes instead of immediately assigning the blame to someone else.

It takes a strong, healthy emotional intelligence to laugh in the face of a threatening situation. When we as parents learn to do that, we gain a different perspective of ourselves and of the threatening person.[6] We all need help to learn how to laugh at ourselves when we make mistakes because that is not what people normally do. If we don't take ourselves too seriously and teach our children to do the same, we will be teaching them a valuable life lesson. Life is all about continuing on in a mature, responsible way after we have made mistakes. If we can teach this to our children, we will be teaching them to be resourceful.

5. Self-regulation. Children, who grow up in homes where parents are responsive to their needs instead of reactive, learn self-regulation much easier. However, we can learn self-control at any age when we are motivated and understand why it is necessary. Learning to control our words and our anger is a discipline that pays dividends. It is also a discipline that has lost favor in our postmodern society.

Many children today aren't expected to be able to rule over their own urges and desires. Responsive parenting teaches them otherwise. Teaching your child how to rule over their emotions, such as anger, is a tool that will prevent them from sabotaging important relationships in the future. Even teaching our children to control their expectations so that they expect a reasonable outcome can help them avoid disappointment.

Self-Worth

When we comprehend God's grace to us and show grace to our children, they feel secure and no longer feel the need to try to prove their worth. They won't feel compelled to strive for a higher status. The overwhelming need to compare themselves to others and justify their worthiness by pointing out the faults of others becomes unnecessary. As a child comprehends how much he is loved and observes your self-control, he will learn the value of his own self-control.

Helping your children have a healthy self-esteem is critically tied to their ability to have self-control. If they do, they will avoid the trap of comparing themselves with others. You will be saving them so much heartache by doing so. All through life our children will be compared to others, but they can learn to be strong enough to refuse to buy into this mentality. Our unconditional acceptance of them and the belief that God made only one of them is their platform to resist comparisons.

Making Meaning out of Chaos

Life has a way of throwing undesirable events into our lives. When people suffer traumatic events, they will suffer intrusive and painful thoughts about the event until they are able to accommodate what happened. In other words, they need to be able to obtain some kind of meaning out of the seemingly meaningless occurrence.

Unfortunately, some people are never able to find meaning in some of the tragedies of their lives. Even though years have passed, they still experience distress from their memories of traumatic events that play back in their brain like a looped video. For others, these intrusive memories work like a domino effect and trigger other feelings of loss or shame. These memories may be so overwhelming that they cause self-destructive acts. We need help to be able to accommodate our bad memories.

Some of our worst memories may have to do with broken relationships, such as when we are cut off from a mother or father. Often, relationships in families can be disastrous because of divorce, conflict, or other problems. Some of the most impressionable relationships have been shipwrecked when a child is at a vulnerable age. Looking back, we often don't even know what really happened. We need help to sort it all out.

On September 5, 1856, the *Arabian*, a steamboat that had traveled the Missouri River for several years, hit a submerged tree stump and sank near Kansas City. The Missouri was notorious for these kinds of dangers. All the passengers survived, but the boat was a total loss until 131 years later when Bob Hawley and his sons found the steamboat half a mile from the river, buried under 45 feet of topsoil. Through elaborate efforts, it was raised with most of its cargo still intact.

Today, it is a fascinating museum to see what was lost for so long and finally rescued. This is what I mean about learning to accommodate and bring meaning out of the tragedies of our lives. Those memories may be buried under years of hurt and resentment, but with the right help, they can be resurrected and accommodated to have meaning. No longer do they just represent tragedy and loss. Instead, you will be able to see something of value through it and not be afraid to talk about what happened because it finally makes sense. Often times what appears to be a total loss in our lives can, with God's grace, be resurrected. God can help us find the treasure in our tragedies.

A wonderful picture of accommodation can be seen in the

word *redemption*. When God redeems us, he accommodates the tragic, shameful, and meaningless events of our lives. Only God has the ultimate power to take whatever we give him and make something meaningful out of it. When Paul wrote to the Ephesians, he said this: "In him we have redemption through his blood, the forgiveness of sins, in accordance with the riches of God's grace" (Eph. 1:7).

Nowhere do we see the price of our redemption clearer than in the sufferings of Jesus. His suffering was colossal and incomparable, but it was to help us accommodate the meaningless transgressions of our lives. Jesus not only suffered for us but also showed us how to suffer. He never lost control and never became resentful or vengeful of those who hurt him. He never let the hurt done to him change him, and he does the same thing for us.

Jesus showed such power and restraint during his suffering. When he was arrested, Peter tried to defend him by cutting off the high priest's servant's ear. Jesus had at his disposal infinite power but declined to fight back. His response to Peter was, "Do you think I cannot call on my Father, and he will at once put at my disposal more than twelve legions of angels?" (Matt. 26:53). Who of us wouldn't have used that power to even things up, but not Jesus because of his focus and self-control.

Peter never forgot that, and in his letters to the church so many years later, he wrote: "When they hurled their insults at him, he did not retaliate; when he suffered, he made no threats. Instead, he entrusted himself to him who judges justly" (1 Pet. 2:23).

How quick we are to defend ourselves when we are attacked. How fast we return insults to those who insult us. Never was there a man who suffered such injustice and yet bore no revenge. Jesus is the One who can teach us how to live, how to suffer, and how to accommodate the tragedies of our lives.

Jesus suffered to redeem us from our sins, but more than that, Jesus takes everything in our lives and remakes it in a way that has meaning and depth. In other words, he takes the seemingly meaningless, tragic events of our lives and accommodates them so that they no longer control us.

In fact, the things that once caused us pain and interfered with our normal lives become meaningful memories because God helps us view them differently. There is nothing in your life that Jesus cannot make sense out of. Paul said it this way, "And God is able to make all grace abound to you, so that in all things at all times, having all that you need, you will abound in every good work" (2 Cor. 9:8).

My daughter related a story to me that made me laugh. As she was driving one day, she heard her three-year-old daughter Caitlin say, "In your happiness, in your madness, in your gladness, in your sadness, in your fearedness, God is with you. God is with you in all your nesses." She may have only been three, but she had that right. No matter what state our emotions are in or in what circumstances we find ourselves, God is with us. He is with us in all our "nesses."

No matter if we are feeling lonely and abandoned, angry and hurt, fearful and afraid, or even excited and happy, God is with us in all our emotions. He made us and knows what we are like. The Apostle Paul, in his first letter to Timothy, gave thanks to God for his marvelous grace. He was thankful that God chose him though he was an unworthy blasphemer who had persecuted Christians. Paul says, "The grace of our Lord was poured out on me abundantly, along with the faith and love that are in Christ Jesus" (1 Tim. 1:14).

Are you aware of how much God's grace has been abundantly poured out on your life? Paul had been a hard, arrogant murderer who was obsessed with hunting down and persecuting Christians. Though he had once been the hunter, God hunted him down, saved him, and called him to be his apostle to the Gentiles. When Paul thought about this, he was lost in the wonder of God's amazing grace.

You may be familiar with the song "Amazing Grace," but are you familiar with the author? His name is John Newton. He was born in London on July 24, 1725. He grew up the son of a merchant captain, so he learned all about the seas. Later, he was drafted into military service, but John's depraved nature surfaced. Eventually he wound up on a slave ship, ultimately becoming a captain of his own ship. He treated people in a deplorable manner and lived as a complete reprobate. He had been abused, so he abused others. It is what happens to most abused people.

He had some early religious instruction from his mother who had died when he was a child, but he long since had given up any religious convictions. However, on one voyage, while John was attempting to steer the ship through a violent storm, he experienced what he was to refer to later as his "great deliverance."

He recorded in his journal that when all seemed lost and the ship would surely sink, he exclaimed, "Lord, have mercy upon us." Later in his cabin, he reflected on what he had said and began to believe that God had addressed him through the storm and grace had begun to work for him. For the rest of his life, he observed the anniversary of May 10, 1748, as the day of his conversion, a day in which he subjected his will to a higher power.[7]

John Newton went on to pen the familiar song that has ministered to so many: "Amazing Grace."

Amazing grace!
How sweet the sound that saved a wretch like me!
I once was lost, but now am found, was blind,
　　but now I see.
'Twas grace that taught my heart to fear,
　　and grace my fears relieved;
How precious did that grace appear
　　the hour I first believed!
("Amazing Grace," John Newton, 1779)

8

When Parents Combine Their Gifts

There are augments written about who makes the greatest contributions to children—the mother or the father. Some experts claim it's the mother of course, and then others single out the fathers. Actually, these arguments are frivolous because both make an indelible mark on the children, but they can have even a bigger influence if they work together and combine their efforts.

There is a direct link between the quality of the relationship between the parents and the quality of their parenting. In other words, if Mom and Dad are on the same page when it comes to parenting, the children will do so much better. Fathers are typically much more involved with their children when they have better relationships with their children's mothers.

When parents have a cooperative parenting style, they support each other and minimize conflict. The higher the incidence of conflict between parents, the lower the cooperation in the parenting style. The opposite is also true; if parents learn to work on their differences and implement conflict resolution, then the children benefit from their efforts.[1]

A child exposed to conflict has an amazing amount of resiliency to overcome distress when conflicts are resolved. What is encouraging is that when we mess up as parents, our children will forgive us if we ask them. Even when parents are divorced, it is essential to put the children's welfare above your own griev-ances against an ex-husband or ex-wife.

Effective Positive Interaction

Effective positive interaction between a child and the parent is the key to proper child and adolescent development. Any in-teraction where the parent plays with a child, follows the child's lead, or interacts with the child reinforces new skills and inter-ests. It would be impossible to overemphasize the importance of playing with your little children. Buying them toys is not nearly as important as Mom and Dad playing with them. The interest a child displays in an activity is largely dependent on the interest others have shown in the child's activity and progress.[2]

Early interactions are the platform for healthy, secure at-tachment, which enables a child to develop his or her mental capacity.[3] When a child forms a secure attachment with the parent, that attachment promotes feelings of self-worth and contributes to positive interactions with other people.[4] Even if the child is not yet two years of age, she knows who her daddy and mommy are. She knows who loves her and who protects her, and she knows who feeds, clothes, and comforts her. That bond that forms first with the mother and then with the father is God-given.

Having a positive interaction with parents is a platform on which the important ideals of a little personality will be built and upon which they will survive. The birth of a child is a sudden realization to the parents of the miracle of life that has been growing in the womb for nine months. However, for par-ents who are fully engaged, a realization of human development continues through each successive stage that they observe in their children. The interaction that started in infancy continues throughout the child's life and into adulthood.

The roles of mothers and fathers complement each other in the parenting process. One parent may be more likely to respond to a child's displays of sadness, but the other may be more responsive to problems with problem solving strategies. Together they show the best qualities of both genders. The father may offer unique contributions with the child's social interaction, while the mother is more emotionally connected during the adolescent years.[5]

When mothers and fathers keep their word to each other and to their children, they teach their children that they are dependable. The result is that their children learn to be responsible. Children need stability, and learning to be responsible is one way to get it. They need to know that Mom and Dad are going to be there no matter what happens. Lewis Smedes' words about keeping promises underscore their importance:

> Yes, somewhere people still make and keep promises. They choose not to quit when the going gets rough because they promised once to see it through. They stick to lost causes. They hold on to a love grown cold. They stay with people who have become pains in the neck. They still dare to make promises and care enough to keep the promises they make. I want to say to you that if you have a ship you will not desert, if you have people you will not forsake, if you have causes you will not abandon, then you are like God. What a marvelous thing a promise is! When a person makes a promise, she reaches out into an unpredictable future and makes one thing predictable: she will be there even when being there costs her more than she wants to pay. When a person makes a promise, he stretches himself

out into circumstances that no one can control and controls at least one thing: he will be there no matter what the circumstances turn out to be. With one simple word of promise, a person creates an island of certainty in a sea of uncertainty. When a person makes a promise, she stakes a claim on her personal freedom and power. When you make a promise, you take a hand in creating your own future.[6]

When fathers keep their promises to their wives and vice versa, the children learn to keep their own promises, first to their parents and then to others around them. The greatest gift a man can give his children is to love their mother or a mother to love their father.

Dealing With Conflict

Research is emphatic in what it says about the effects of exposure to unresolved conflict on children, such as marital discord and reactive parenting. The resounding evidence points out repeatedly that children exposed to continual conflict are at an elevated risk of depression, aggressive behavioral problems, and lack of self-regulation, along with defensive behavioral tendencies in adolescence and adulthood.[7] Reactive parenting focuses on putting out fires and is always dealing with problems. Whatever the source, the parenting inevitably evolves into a negative parenting style that fosters negative emotion.

Responsive parenting, on the other hand, is deliberate and thoughtful. It demonstrates emotional control that rises above the reactive interaction that can happen because of irritability or temperament. This style of parenting offers the child much needed emotional availability and warmth and provides the atmosphere in which children flourish.[8]

The relationship between Mom and Dad is genuine and loving, which draws in the children. The relationship that each parent establishes with the children provides the means to enrich and influence their lives. The structure and focus is on being the right person—the person you were meant to be. This frees children from performance driven behavior.

Approachable

Children need parents who are approachable no matter what the situation. They need to know that they will be heard and the parent will make an informed decision about their complaints and questions. Most of us can remember some situation we faced growing up when we didn't feel there was any accessibility. When I was in the sixth grade, I was asked to try out for the school choir. I was all nerves when the music teacher called me to the piano where he was sitting with all my peers watching. Each person was supposed to sing a couple of lines as he played. Several in front of me sang on key and were praised for their abilities. When I sang I was told, "Go back to class; we don't need you."

It was one of those shameful moments I never forgot. That teacher created a moment that lived in my memory as an unapproachable moment. When parents are approachable, they are keenly aware of what the child is feeling and do not want the child to experience shame. If the child is embarrassed, they do what is necessary to give a different meaning to that awkward moment.

Here is an example of responsive parenting versus reactive. Let's say that a fourteen-year-old girl comes home from school very upset. She throws her book bag down, doesn't speak to her parents, goes straight to her room, and slams the door. The reactive parents follow her to the room and demand an explanation for her behavior, which produces an argument. Finally, the authoritarian parent lays down the law and says that there will be no more of that kind of disrespect, and the incident is over. At least it is over to the reactive parent.

The responsive parents go to the room and ask the girl what happened to make her so upset. Even if she is reluctant to talk, they wait and coax her into sharing. When they find out that something terribly embarrassing has happened to her, they comfort her and help her make meaning out of the whole ordeal. They help her express her emotions and experience some relief. They tell her how much they love her and care about her, but they also let her know that in the future, even though she may be upset, she cannot show disrespect for them the way she did. She apologizes, and they make a connection. The difference between the two approaches is like day and night.

The impact of growing up in a home where there is minimal conflict, and the conflict that exists gets resolved, is extremely beneficial to the children. Children who have a model of respectful interaction exhibit less defensiveness. Less defensive behavior translates into better interpersonal communication and more meaningful relationships.[9] One way of illustrating this is to imagine making emotional deposits into our children's lives. Mothers and fathers who work together do that consistently.

Appreciating the Differences

- God made complementary roles for men and women because they are so different.

- Their unique differences give each one certain advantages and gifts the other does not have or at least does not have in the same capacity.

- Most women are gifted with more relational connection that seems to be instinctual, which allows them to have quicker insight into their children's emotional lives.

- Most men project more physical strength simply because they are bigger and stronger, and they are made that way.

- When it comes to parenting, those differences and many more become extremely valuable.

- The mother will be invaluable in her mothering instincts, and the father will be appreciated for his ability to bring direction and discipline.

- It all functions so much better when they work together and not against each other.

One of the most important discoveries of marriage and parenting is to come to appreciate the differences of your husband or wife. Many couples focus on the faults of the other and even exaggerate those flaws to their children. When we get to the place where we completely accept our spouse and their unique personality, we are on the road to a meaningful relationship and responsive parenting.

We won't always be able do that because we are all flawed, but God gave us a wonderful gift called forgiveness. It restores the balance by promoting the resolution of the conflict through healing the hurts and giving us a greater understanding of the causes of the conflict. This understanding can lead to a determination to resolve further conflict.

Parenting Together

- Responsive parenting that is thoughtful and dedicated to doing the right thing fosters higher levels of self-esteem and maturity in the children.

- When there is open communication in the home between the parents and the children, the children obtain higher levels of autonomy and acquire life skills that will help them throughout adult life.

- When the mother and father are connected, they bring a united front to their parenting, and there will be fewer behavioral problems in the children.

- When the children feel loved and accepted, they are more inclined to internalize the parent's values and attitudes.

- When parents work to resolve conflict and explain their actions, children are able to concentrate, maintain their focus, function better academically, and are generally happier.[10]

We have all felt so proud and excited as our children performed in some public event. It probably wasn't that they acted so much better, played their instruments so much better, or said their lines with more eloquence than others, but it was because of our connection with them: "That's my son or my daughter up there!" It was the relationship that gave significance to the moment. The greater the connection between husband and wife, the greater effectiveness of their parenting.

The prophet Amos stated the principle of teamwork like this: "Do two walk together unless they have agreed to do so?" (Amos 3:3). Solomon said it this way,

Two are better than one, because they have a good return for their work: If one falls down, his friend can help him up. But pity the man who falls and has no one to help him up! Also, if two lie down together, they will keep warm. But how can one keep warm alone? Though one may be overpowered, two can defend themselves. A cord of three strands is not quickly broken" (Eccl. 4:9-12).

This principle of unity is true in every field, but in parenting it is essential because children feel the tension or the unity of their parents.

Responsive parenting is about capturing the moment and realizing that these are crucial years. Moses' mother, Jocobed, realized this when she was given the opportunity by Pharaoh's daughter to raise her baby boy for the first few years of his life.

> *"Take this baby and nurse him for me, and I will pay you." So the woman took the baby and nursed him. When the child grew older, she returned him to Pharaoh's daughter and he became her son. She named him Moses, saying, "I drew him out of the water"* (Ex. 2:8-10).

Each parent may have a more dominant role for a season than the other. When one parent is playing an important role, the other is supportive and vice versa. The key here, though, is that both parents are standing together in the process.

- When both parents are really involved in the parenting process, it becomes responsive instead of reactive.
- Both parents are able to create an atmosphere of positive control where the children learn that the parents are actually in control and respect that authority.
- There is no playing Mom against Dad because they are on the same team. Mom and Dad set limits and teach their children in an environment of warmth and acceptance.
- When both parents are actively involved in raising the child, the positive outcomes for the child are much higher.

In a healthy family any child is inevitably going to see some conflict. The important point is not whether the child sees some conflict, but whether the child sees conflict resolution. The child is most likely not harmed by exposure to some conflict but can actually benefit when he or she learns from it.[11] It's all about what the parents do or do not do with the conflict in their family.

Integration of Core Values

When parents understand their core values and are consistent in their daily interactions, then those values will be integrated in the child's life. When parents take ownership for their own lives and demonstrate to the child what they believe, it will make sense to the child or adolescent.[12]

- The real integration of core values depends on the quality of the relationship between the youth and the parents.

- A warm, connected parent is associated with fewer problem behaviors in their adolescent.

- Adolescents who receive more parental warmth tend to engage less in antisocial behavior and more in positive behavior.

- When adolescents feel valued, accepted, and loved, they are far more inclined to internalize parental values and accept their parents' rules and attitudes.[13]

The quality of parenting also has an impact on whether the children raised in the home will appropriate the religious and spiritual beliefs and practices of the parents.

I remember how the task of teaching my daughter, Carin, to ride a bike was not the easiest task in the world. She would do all right as long as she knew my hand was on the back of the bike. If she ever looked back and saw that I had taken my hand off or that I had stopped running behind her, she would tumble over. We had so many crashes because of that. After many tries, I decided to get her started and run ahead of her so that she would follow me, and it worked. The results were immediate. I became her goal on which she could focus, and in so doing, she was able to keep her balance.

Throughout their childhood, children need to be able to look up and see us leading the way so they can follow. If you become distracted for several months here or there, your children will have an emotional crash. When you project your strength and affirm your love for them regularly, they will keep going and make forward progress.

9

Combating Shame
With Acceptance

Everyone experiences shaming situations in life because we live in an imperfect world. The worst kind of shame is when it is associated with our own personal worth and accomplishments. The shaming experience makes us feel we are not worth nearly as much as we thought we were because of the obvious rejection we feel. Then once shame takes hold, it can hijack control of the rest of our lives.

None of us are spared from experiencing shame, even very famous people. General Ulysses S. Grant, after graduating from West Point with the rank of Second Lieutenant, was feeling pretty good about his accomplishment. He was eager to wear his new tailored uniform so old schoolmates and particularly the girls could be impressed. But that is not how things turned out. When Grant rode into Cincinnati in his new uniform with his sword dangling at his side, he expected to be admired. Instead, he was ridiculed. The shame sent a powerful message to Grant's psyche that he didn't matter. Throughout the remainder of his career, he would go to great lengths to avoid wearing full service dress, and he never wore a sword unless ordered.[1]

I can identify with this experience in Grant's life because I can still remember the day I opened my first bank account with

"Reverend" in front of my name. The woman across the desk asked, "This must be a mistake?" Her words were spoken in an incredulous tone because I was so young. I had completed my first step toward the ministerial license, but I still looked like a kid. However, the incident caused me never to use the word Reverend again with my name though I am an ordained minister. I recovered from the shame of that incident and chose to go by Pastor, but the sting of that encounter is still in my memory.

We all have these kinds of experiences that shape our lives and in some cases actually sabotage our future and the quality of our interaction with people. Our self-esteem plummets, and we withdraw, giving in to the message that we are so much less than we ever thought we were. Although most people overcome their shaming experiences, others deal with the effects of them all their lives.[2]

Shame often causes a person to feel small, with a sense of worthlessness and powerlessness. Shamed people often feel that they are exposed and that what has happened to them is obvious to everyone. Their shame can lead to depression, self-destructive behavior, and isolation.[3] Others who have been shamed will react with a heightened sense of anger and will often blame others. This reaction rarely offers relief, but it is their way of saying, "I may be messed up, but it's not my fault."[4]

When parents realize how impressionable their children are, they do everything they can to spare them the experience of shame. And if shame does occur, they help them understand what happened to them and overcome it. If parents do that, children have a much greater possibility of leading a stable, adult life. For those who experience shame and carry it with them into adult life, God can heal their brokenness.

The best antidote for such appalling experiences is in the

healing presence of God. Isaiah the prophet said that we are saved through repentance and quietly learning to trust God. It is a process where we slowly get strong enough to overcome such devastating experiences. Though we may have been shamed and the hurt still lingers, God longs to show us grace and compassion (Isaiah 30:15-18). As destructive as shame is, it is never beyond the reach of God's grace.

Self-Esteem

How important is our self-esteem? Pretty important when you consider that many people we meet on a daily basis are very insecure. Maybe you remember a man who kept recounting his exploits so everyone would be impressed or the woman who never let anyone else talk. They were both trying to earn approval from people because of their insecurities. Most of us can remember some situation we faced growing up when we experienced a powerful, shaming experience.

We get most of our confidence in the first three years of our lives from the loving bond with Mom and Dad. Something wonderful happens in a child's life when she realizes that she is loved unconditionally. However, we can only get another part of that self-esteem from God. He is our Creator, and we long for his affirmation until we are secure in him.

As secure and unconditional as the love we receive from our parents is, it can never hold a light to God's unconditional love for each of us. He loves us despite our faults and shortcomings, and he never changes his love. He loves us even when we are unworthy of his love. No matter when we come to God, he is ready and willing to embrace us with his love.

I once played a little game with one of my two-year-old granddaughters. I would say, "Are you Grandpa's girl?" She usually answered, "No, I'm Grandma's girl" or "I'm Mommy's girl." I responded by saying, "What!" and she giggled. One night, however, at an outside barbecue she came up to me said, "Grandpa, can I hold you?" I, of course, picked her up and sat her down on my lap, and we had some Cheez-Its. I asked her, "Whose girl are you?" She responded, "Grandpa's girl." I very well knew that the next time Grandma or Mommy appeared that would change, but it never kept me from loving my little granddaughter when she asked to be held.

Likewise, when we come to God, regardless of the reason, he never questions the motive but extends his loving arms to us. In fact, that is what Jesus said:

> *Come to me, all you who are weary and burdened, and I will give you rest. Take my yoke upon you and learn from me, for I am gentle and humble in heart, and you will find rest for your souls. For my yoke is easy and my burden is light* (Matt. 11:28-30).

No matter how old your children are, if you make time for them and a place for them in your life, you will be helping them grow. The acceptance and love they receive from you is what makes them strong enough to overcome the shaming experiences they will receive as they grow older. No matter who tells them they are not special—they know differently because of all the occasions when you have shown them unconditional love and acceptance. You are building in them an unassailable self-esteem. However, the greatest gift you give them is to introduce them to Jesus and allow him to be real to them.

Some things in life need our constant attention. A garden won't grow healthy fruits and vegetables or flowers without the constant care of a good gardener. Someone has to do the work of tending to the garden if you want the plants to flourish.

Sometimes there are weeds to pull or dead branches to trim, but always there is the job of watering and caring for the plants.

Important relationships are like that. They only flourish in our lives when we tend to them. Things happen, like misunderstandings, and hurt feelings can be the result. Someone has to take the initiative to mend the relationship. If the marriage relationship is left unattended, husbands and wives will drift apart; hurt unattended will separate the closest of friends.

We have to find a way to get across the barriers and restore the relationship when it breaks down. Our marriages and our families are worth the sacrifice. When we have done wrong, then by all means we must be quick to apologize and ask forgiveness. Life is simply too short to live another day without restoring the relationships that really matter in our lives. We need to let God intervene for us today; he will carry us across the divide and reunite us with our family members. God will help you reconnect if you are willing to ask for his help.

Made for Connection

On Christmas Day 1989, the Communist Romanian dictator Nicolae Ceausescu and his wife, Elena, were executed by a firing squad. This man was one of the world's most evil dictators who has ever lived. For almost 25 years he ruled Romania with an iron fist and eliminated his enemies without tolerating a word of protest. He brought incredible poverty and misery upon his nation, while he and his wife lived in opulent luxury.

He demanded of the Romanians that they have huge families to populate their country. At the same time he established state run orphanages to accommodate all the abandoned children that started appearing. When the country fell apart, there were over 100,000 children in orphanages.

Growing up in a loving home where parents give you more than food and shelter is essential to proper brain development. These Romanian children from the orphanages proved that when a child does not have someone in their little life to give them attention and stimulate their brain—brain growth is stunted. The long-term result is cognitive and emotional problems.

Dr. Nathan Fox, professor at the University of Maryland, conducted a longitudinal study with the children growing up in these Romanian orphanages. The study revealed changes in the brain composition of these kids who spent their first years there versus those who were randomly assigned to foster care. The findings pointed to a sensitive period in the brain for social development.[5]

The evidence clearly shows that early childhood experiences can have lasting impacts on the brain. Traumatic neglect on a child may shrink regions in the brain. Dr. Ziegler writes, "Neglectful conditions produce deprivation of the brain precisely at a time when it is prepared to make the most significant gains in adapting to the new environment."[6]

Fox found these orphanages were understaffed, abuse was rampant, and neglect was a way of life. Conditions were very regimented—they all had to eat, bathe, and go to the toilet at the same time. There was very little training for caregivers and a very bad ratio of caregivers to children.[7]

The study also revealed that the brains of the children in the orphanages lost gray matter volume. In addition, a lower quality brain activity was measured by EEG, and kids were also more distant socially. The difference between those in the orphanages and those in homes was remarkable. The kids' behavior and brain activity from homes suggest how warmly and securely bonded they were to their main caregiver. The idea is that those kids who develop a secure attachment actually show enhanced brain activity.[8]

There is a special window for a child to be stimulated emotionally and intellectually by her parents. If that happens, the brain develops; and if it doesn't, odd behaviors will result. The child will have difficulty interacting with other people. Motor skills, language, and personality development will be delayed. The brain activity of such children is diminished, and even the physical size of the brain will be smaller.[9]

When a little baby, and later a toddler, feels secure and is stimulated by his parents and family members, something vital happens. From that interaction the baby's brain grows, and out of that growth everything about that child will be affected positively in some way or another. These primary years are so important for parents to enjoy and for the children to flourish. If the parents are fighting and not available, they not only lose these years but also render a disservice to the child.

At one point we had to put one of our sons in a daycare when he was about two and were apprehensive as to how he would do. His first day he cried his eyes out. The second day we took him, we were expecting the same scene. However, to our surprise, when we reached the gate he looked around and spotted the person he was looking for and took off. I stood there for a moment and watched as parents brought their children, and most of the kids were running to the same person.

This woman was a plump little lady who was hugging and squeezing the kids. I wondered what it was that made so many of the kids run to her. I noticed other workers all by themselves with no kids running to them. Over the next few weeks, it wasn't hard to figure out why the kids took to this lady. She had something to give them. She had a certain grace about her that made it so easy for every child in the daycare to connect to her.

During World War II, Allied pilots returning from bombing raids on the oil fields in Romania were forced to bail out over Yugoslavia. Over time, hundreds of pilots were found and protected by the villagers and the soldiers of Yugoslavian General Mihailovich. These soldiers suffered from little food and a lack of medical attention, but they found the worst part of the experience was that they were disconnected from their units. In August 1944, the Allied Air Force organized a secret mission consisting of C-47s that flew in under cover of dozens of fighter planes and rescued 512 airmen.[10]

Just as those airmen longed to be reconnected to their units, so couples who are cut off from each other in their marriages long for reconnection. The same longing happens with children and parents. We all long for connection. When traumatic things happen in families like death or divorce, families have to find a way to compensate for the loss by connecting. If not, the loss will take its toll on the children in later years.

People were made by God for connection, and this connection was meant to begin in the earliest stages of our lives. It's exciting to see young parents enthusiastic about parenting. How enjoyable it is to see them playing and interacting with their small children. Just as a phone searches for the network when you turn it on, people are always searching for connection. Something incredibly wonderful happens when parents interact in a positive way with their little children.

Many problems have one root cause—an emotional disconnection with the person or persons they love. When a husband and wife lose their connection, they are going to experience difficulties. If they don't recognize what is happening and go to work on it immediately, there will be consequences. When a couple has to deal with the pain of an affair, it is a horrible experience. They must decide, however, if they will work for connection or let the pain separate them for good.

What is so important for them to discover is that the affair was the culmination of their emotional disconnection—not the beginning. Disconnections always begin in simple ways, such as that of not doing the kind and loving things for each other that characterize connected relationships. However, they also include an element of betrayal. Brene Brown has capably written on this subject in a fine book entitled *Daring Greatly*:

> When the people we love or with whom we have a deep connection stop caring, stop paying attention, stop investing, and stop fighting for the relationship, trust begins to slip away and hurt starts seeping in. Disengagement triggers shame and our greatest fears— the fears of being abandoned, unworthy, and unlovable. What can make this covert betrayal so much more dangerous than something like a lie or an affair is that we can't point to the source of our pain— there's no event, no obvious evidence of brokenness.[11]

Every person who knows the genuine satisfaction of being connected to another person in a loving relationship (the best example of this is marriage) also knows the work of guarding that connection. There are a host of things that can erode that connection: work, sickness, depression, disappointment or just the unpredictability of life. Healthy relationships stay healthy because the people stay connected.

Staying connected doesn't happen by accident but rather because two people choose to make it happen every day of their lives. That same connection extends to the children and binds the family together. Whenever a disconnection happens, and it will, family members have to work at reconnecting no matter how difficult it is. The problem is not in the disconnection, but in the failure to work at it and put things right. When couples feel their relationship is stagnated and they don't know what to do, then they need help and should seek it.

Stay Connected

Several years ago while living in Argentina, I left my family for the evening to attend a church service some twenty miles away. I drove across a bridge that spanned the Paraná River. When I returned, the bridge was closed, and I couldn't get home. Though I was only a little over a mile away and could actually see my neighborhood, I was cut off from my family.

I walked to a little fishing village up stream and inquired if there were any fishermen who had an available boat to take me across. It took a while, but I finally found someone. The *mayonero*, as they are called, had certainly consumed one too many drinks, so I was a little apprehensive as to whether or not he would really get me across. As we were making our way across the mammoth river, I noticed a substantial amount of water getting in the boat. I asked the man, "Aren't you worried about the water in the boat?" He replied, "No, it can handle twice that much before we sink."

The trip across the river seemed like it took forever, but we finally arrived on the other side, and I disembarked right in the middle of a beach party. People stared at me as I got out of the fishing boat, wearing a suit and carrying a brief case, but it didn't matter because I would be home in a few short minutes and reunited with my family.

When we find ourselves cut off from a wife or husband or a

son or daughter, it's time to act. If for some unexpected reason the path to clear communication is closed, there is an awkward feeling and estrangement. It is precisely in that moment that we need to find a way to get across the barriers and restore the relationship. Our marriage, our sons, and our daughters are worth the sacrifice. We have to work hard at finding out what has come between us and let them know how much we value the relationship. If we have done something wrong, then by all means we must be quick to apologize and ask forgiveness.

Life is simply too short to live another day without restoring the relationships that really matter in our lives. Many times the hurt is so great that we need God to intervene. God will help, but we have to be willing to ask for his help. Whatever it takes, we need to find a way to get across the barriers and reconnect with our family. Sometimes it means finding someone to help take us across the uncharted waters of reconciliation. Whatever it takes, it is worth the effort.

Acceptance Builds Relationship

The lion who wanted to prove his authority asked a bear, "Who is the king of the jungle?" The bear answered, "You, of course!" Having heard what he wanted to hear, he then asked a tiger, "Who is the king of the jungle?" The tiger answered, "You, of course!" Again having heard what he wanted to hear, he then asked an elephant, "Who is the king of the jungle?" The elephant grabbed him and threw him up in the air and let him fall on some rocks. Grasping him again he threw him higher than ever and let him fall into some trees. The lion, now bruised and limping, replied to the elephant, "If you don't know the right answer, you don't have to get so mad about it."

We all want to be accepted and validated, but it is amazing

how hard it is for us to give that acceptance to others. We expect affirmation and praise while rarely returning it. Instead, like the lion, we often seek to assert our authority over others no matter what. The Bible explains why we do this: "...for all have sinned and fall short of the glory of God" (Rom. 3:23). Unless we learn to let God's grace intervene, our selfish natures will insist on our being first at any cost. Remember this selfish nature will manifest itself in our toddlers. Every child has to be taught to be kind and accepting of others. Sharing doesn't come naturally; we have to be taught.

The Apostle Paul is an example of someone who had the ability to accept other people who were different than he was and encourage them. He certainly wasn't always that way, but God's marvelous grace transformed him. When Paul wrote Timothy his second letter from a Roman prison, the last letter he would ever write, he was very much alone and very lonely. The letter is very personal and was meant to encourage and inspire Timothy.

Paul was the complete opposite of Timothy. He was an extrovert and Timothy an introvert. He was as bold as a lion and Timothy as fearful as a frightened kitten, and yet Paul gently accepts these differences in Timothy. His words here to Timothy were uplifting:

> *For this reason I remind you to fan into flame the gift of God, which is in you through the laying on of my hands. For God did not give us a spirit of timidity, but a spirit of power, of love and of self-discipline* (2 Tim. 1:6-7).

We need that same kind of ability to accept the differences in each of our children and encourage them.

Acceptance of another person is a mature act that changes

both people. The greater the acceptance of each other in marriage, the more satisfying the relationship will be. Take, for example, a husband who has trouble because his wife is very outgoing and has many friends, while he is very solitary. He criticizes her and tries to change her into an introvert like himself. It won't work, and it will diminish her self-esteem and weaken their relationship.

When he recognizes (and this may take years) that this is how God made her and he accepts her as she is, he begins to see how she blossoms when she is free to be herself. He then will begin to enjoy his relationship with her more than he ever imagined. Perhaps the same could be said about the wife who nags her husband because he is such a spendthrift and doesn't like spending money. The more she tries to change him into a spender like herself, the more unhappy he is and the more the relationship is diminished. Only when she begins to see his ways as helpful, do the both of them begin to enjoy each other.

This concept is applicable to every human relationship. When you see the unique differences in your children and accept them, only then are you able to build on their strengths and minimize their weaknesses.

10

Resolving Conflict

The perfect family does not exist. All families have problems and have to deal with conflict because we are flawed human beings. However, the way families deal with conflict impacts every child in a way that affects the rest of their life. Children who see conflict on a regular basis, such as Mom and Dad fighting, Mom and daughter yelling, or Dad and son competing against each other, are placed in a precarious situation. If they don't see some resolution to the conflict, they will begin to internalize the negative emotions or very possibly act them out. These children need the mom and dad to call everyone together and talk the conflict out in order to bring resolution the entire family can see and experience.

When children grow up in a family where the mom and dad talk things out and handle conflict in a calm, resolute way, the children learn how to handle their emotions. When they hear apologies and see firsthand Mom or Dad say they're sorry and ask forgiveness, then they learn how to do that themselves. This vital skill will be needed later in life and is essential to building meaningful relationships. We aren't capable of living perfect lives—we will inevitably make mistakes, and what we need is a means of restoring broken communication and broken relationships by learning to apologize and forgive.

Often families identify a difficult member of the family as

the "real problem," such as a rebellious adolescent or a depressed mom, but in a family everyone is part of the problem. If you had a bicycle repair shop and someone brought you a broken spoke and asked you to fix the bicycle, you would respond by asking, "Where is the rest of the bike?" Families often do this as they focus on one member of the family as the problem, often completely oblivious to the fact that the problem involves the entire family.

When families avoid talking about problems, they create deeper problems. When they tackle any problem head on, whether it is a bad attitude or out of control emotions, they are helping everyone in the family bring clarity out of confusion. Clarity is what we all want and need to keep us together and understand each other better.

When families avoid talking about issues they have, they are allowing the problems to get bigger, but they are also failing to equip the children with the needed skills to solve their own problems. When we observe a problem in our children or ourselves, we must talk about it, regardless of whether they want to talk about it or not. This is always difficult when a family is not used to talking out their problems. The more they talk and seek resolution, the more accustomed the family becomes to solving problems, which is what every child needs to see.

The Power of Forgiveness

God has given us the most effective tool for resolving conflicts, and it is called forgiveness. The minute we forgive, things start to change and improve, even if it is only you who are doing the forgiving. Failing to forgive brings grave consequences. Vengeful feelings, for example, can flood the brain with toxic chemicals, which happens when we think malicious thoughts or experience strong negative emotion. Researchers describe the results of these chemicals that are released as burning tunnels into the branches of our nerve cells. Amazingly enough, however, when people forgive and begin to heal, so do the black holes in the brain. New memories can replace the old. And one of the virtues neuroscientist Dr. Leaf identifies as bringing the most healing is forgiveness.[1]

One of my favorite authors is Lewis Smedes; he writes about the importance of forgiveness in a book entitled *Forgive & Forget*:

> The point is that hate's searing flame coexists with love's soothing flow; the hate that pushes us apart lives inside us right along with the love that pulls us together. Indeed, we can hate most painfully the people we love most passionately.
>
> Hate eventually needs healing. Passive or aggressive, hate is a malignancy; it is dangerous—deadly, if allowed to run its course. Nothing good comes from a hate that has a person in its sights; and it surely hurts the hater more that it hurts the hated.
>
> We must not confuse hate with anger. It is hate and not anger that needs healing. Anger is a sign that we are alive and well. Hate is a sign that we are sick and need to be healed. Healthy anger drives us to do something to change what makes us angry; anger can energize us to make things better. Hate does not want to change things for the better; it wants to make things worse. Hate wants to belch the foul breath of death over a life that love alone creates.[2]

Forgiveness just might be the best way to control our attitude. Most likely we need to be forgiven and to forgive on a regular basis. Forgiveness is the lubrication that keeps our relationships in working order. Many people, however, haven't learned to use it as often as they should. There are simply too many hurts and consequently too many broken relationships. We can miss opportunities to restore broken lives through the power of forgiveness.

Art Linkletter missed out on a chance to get in on helping finance Disney World in the same way another financier overlooked the opportunity to sell the world Velcro. Both of these proved to be incredible, missed opportunities. Unless we are focused, we will regularly miss crucial opportunities to connect to our spouses and our children. When we talk about missed opportunities, it helps us become more aware of these special moments that happen to each of us.

Jesus' disciples missed an opportunity to minister to their Lord on the night of the Last Supper (John 13:1-14). They all came into the room where they saw the water and the towel, but there were no servants to wash their feet, so they moved on to the table. When Jesus came in, he gave no orders to wash everyone's feet, nor did he rebuke them for not taking care of this task, but he did prepare to do it himself. He took off his mantel and wrapped the towel around his waist. Then, one by one, he washed each disciple's feet. When Jesus finished, he asked his disciples if they comprehended what he had just done.

> *He said to them: "You call me 'Teacher' and 'Lord,' and rightly so, for that is what I am. Now that I, your Lord and Teacher, have washed your feet, you also should wash one another's feet"* (John 13:13-14).

He really caught the disciples by surprise because I think they were expecting him to say that he wanted his feet washed, but he didn't. If you notice, Jesus' feet never got washed—it was a missed opportunity. Any one of them, if they had grabbed the water and towel, could have washed Jesus' feet in the beginning, but it was too late.

Learning To Focus on Others

Jesus used this moment to help them learn to focus on others. They had focused on themselves and had missed an opportunity to minister to Jesus. If, however, they watched what he did and learned to take on his attitude, they could minister to other people the way he did.

Being a good parent is really about learning to be the best person you were meant to be—authenticity minus any hypocrisy. Notice I didn't say perfection, just authenticity! We will gain authenticity by following Jesus' example.

There is no greater opportunity afforded to us in life than to connect to our children while they are growing up. That connection can have a phenomenal influence on them and stays alive if we work at it and if there are others working at staying connected to us. Henry Cloud has written a fine book entitled *The Power of the Other*. He describes that connection like this:

> Relationship affects our physical and mental functioning throughout life. This invisible power, the power of the other, builds both the hardware and the software that leads to healthy functioning and better performance. For example, research shows over and over again that people trying to reach goals succeed at a much greater rate if they are connected to a strong human support system.[3]

That human support system is called a family. When a family values and serves each other, something wonderful happens. In this kind of family, the members are not fighting for position or power but supporting each other.

Only One Superman

One of the obsessions of Hollywood is the creation of a Superman. They have been trying to do this since they started making films, and they are still trying. However, the best they can do is still only fiction. In the original series, Superman would always have to confront the bad guys. In desperation they would pull out their guns and fire at him, which only made Superman smirk and throw his chest out because the bullets would simply bounce off his man-of-steel torso. However, the producers and actors of the series never realized what mistake they did next until it was pointed out later.

When the bad guys ran out of bullets, they would throw their guns at Superman, and he would instinctively duck. Can you believe that? Bullets couldn't hurt him, but when a gun was thrown at him, he ducked. No matter how hard we try to create super-humans, our superman will always duck because we know deep down we are only pretending. There is, however, one person who never has to duck—God!

The prophet Isaiah asks us if we have thought about who God is lately,

Do you not know? Have you not heard? The Lord is the everlasting God, the Creator of the ends of the earth. He will not grow tired or weary, and his understanding no one can fathom" (Isaiah 40:28).

Our God is eternal. He is the one who created everything, including us. He never gets tired or becomes vulnerable because of weakness. His omniscient knowledge is so beyond our understanding. No enemy, no weapon, no disaster, no interruption, nor any kind of problem will ever cause God to duck. Knowing who God is and how powerful he is changes us and is why the prophet wrote such eloquent words to describe God's power and character for us. Isaiah says God not only never ducks in the face of adversity, but he also gives us power to overcome it.

He gives strength to the weary and increases the power of the weak. Even youths grow tired and weary, and young men stumble and fall; but those who hope in the Lord will renew their strength (Isaiah 40:29-30).

Isaiah says this transformation happens for those who put their trust in the Lord. Don't settle for an imitation Superman. There are plenty of impostors out there, but there is only one who is omnipotent, and his name is God! He will pick you up and enable you to do what you could not do on your own. Isaiah continues,

They will soar on wings like eagles; they will run and not grow weary, they will walk and not be faint (Isaiah 40:31).

Our greatest strength is not accomplishing the impossible; it's putting our hope in the One who makes all things possible.

Unresolved conflict in the life of your child is like the static on a poorly tuned radio station. The static is so bothersome that the message isn't clear, and you want to turn it off. Your children need to experience resolution in the normal family conflicts and develop closer relationships. Only then will they truly hear the message.

11

Don't Ever Quit!

Whatever you do, don't quit! Don't quit on your marriage, no matter how hard it gets. Marriage gets rough at times, and it may seem like it's not worth the effort it takes to keep it going. I know so many couples who gave in to discouragement only to regret that decision for the rest of their life. Believe me, it is worth it. You can overcome whatever hurts and whatever mistakes have been made if you work at it.

First, get help for your marriage—don't be ashamed to seek it. Every marriage would benefit from counseling. Then get help for your parenting skills through counseling, reading good books, and talking to people who are older and whom you admire. Look at how their kids turned out and ask them what they did. The people who could really help you aren't going to give you advice unless you ask for it; the people who readily share their advice with you probably shouldn't. Share your struggles with someone who really cares about you and will pray for you.

Don't give up on your kids no matter how difficult it gets. Never stop praying for them and loving them. If you don't give up on them, they won't give up on you. The fact that you are there for them year after year even when they mess up gives them hope and confidence. That is what we call unconditional love. At one time or another, every parent feels like a failure. The only difference between the responsible and irresponsible parent is one thing—the responsible parent does not quit loving, no matter what!

Admitting Wrongs

When we as parents make mistakes or when we allow sin in our lives, we compromise our ability to be good parents. If we want to keep our marriage and our kids on the right track, we have to deal with the wrong in our lives. We have to be honest and completely authentic with our husband or wife and our entire family. Simply put, that means we have to repent and make things right with God and anyone else involved.

I learned this lesson very early in life when I discovered how difficult it is to cover up sin. My older brother, a cousin, and I chose our neighbor's chickens as live targets. We used our 22 caliber rifle to pick them off at close range. After we had killed close to a dozen of those poor creatures, we were faced with how we would hide our crime. We chose the same method as Moses, that of burying them in the sandy soil. At first it looked as if our scheme had worked. However, to our complete dismay, the neighbor's dogs unearthed a great meal for themselves and at the same time uncovered the whole dastardly deed. Our crime began to unravel at breakneck speed. I'll never forget the day I looked up and saw the troubled neighbor coming to our house.

The conversation at the door with my mother went like this, "Mrs. Brooks, my dogs have uncovered nearly a dozen chickens that have been shot and buried. Would your boys have any idea what happened?"

She answered, "I don't know, but I will find out."

She first asked my brother who didn't know a thing of course. Then she honed in on me, and I was a complete pushover and confessed the whole crime, even though I had been threatened that if I told, I too would suffer the same fate as the chickens. The load of concealing this sin any longer was too much to bear.

My mother proceeded to give me and my brother her best and hardest spanking, but the worst part was when she said, "You stay here in your room until your father comes home, and he will really give you something to remember." And he did.

My father drove a truck, so I could hear the truck when it came home. I could hear the gears shifting, the motor being turned off, my mother informing my father, and the door knob turning. Suddenly I was staring at my father.

My father believed in corporal punishment, and although he rarely ever spanked us, the few times he did were crucial for our development. Added to the spanking was the humiliation of going over and apologizing to the neighbor and working to make restitution to pay the man in full for his loss. It certainly seemed like a dumb idea when it was all over. Unquestionably, I would tell anyone never try to bury dead chickens in the dirt when there are dogs in the vicinity.

My brother did, however, teach me a lesson that day. Later, he said as only he could say, "Hey, dummy, don't you know how to take your medicine the right way?" My brother had a real way with words. He went on to explain that when I tried to run away from my father when he was giving me my spanking, it was causing myself more pain. However, if I could learn, as he had, to embrace my father, his swing would be shortened and therefore not hurt nearly as much. It was true.

Even though at the time I dreaded the discipline I received from my father, as I got older I came to appreciate what he did for me. The writer of Hebrews says,

Our fathers disciplined us for a little while as they thought best; but God disciplines us for our good, that we may share in his holiness. No discipline seems pleasant at the time, but painful. Later on, however, it produces a harvest of righteousness and peace for those who have been trained by it (Heb. 12:10-11).

If we run to God when he disciplines us, we will spare ourselves so much agony. God loves us, and everything he does for us is for his glory, and he wants us to be more like him.

Fight for Your Family

When you get the first indication that someone or something is trying to steal your children, fight for them. If they are being influenced by the wrong crowd, if they are defiant and disobedient, if they are experimenting with drugs or alcohol, then go after them. They are yours, and God gave them to you. Every responsible parent should fight for his family.

When things get distorted, we go to the person who can help us get it right. When our car is in an accident, we go to the auto body shop; when the roof leaks, we find a roofer. But who do we go to when we find our purpose in life has been distorted? The answer is Jesus.

We were created in God's image, and as such intended to live out God's purposes in our lives. However, Satan, God's enemy, is filled with hatred for God and tries to distort God's purposes in his creation. What better place to do that than in people—the apex of God's creation. Whether people today believe in such things as a devil and his demons is debatable, but it is not debatable in the Bible. Jesus clearly had power and authority over them.

After the night when Jesus calmed the storm, he and his

disciples landed on the opposite shore. There they met a scary looking and even stranger acting man who wore no clothes and lived in a graveyard (Luke 8:26-39). The reason behind his bizarre behavior was that he was demon possessed.

The poor man's existence was miserable. He cried out and cut himself in an attempt to get relief from the unclean spirits that controlled him. No doubt he had infections and chronic pain from the constant torturing of his own body. Like a wild animal, the man was naked, filthy, unrestrainable, and frightening to anyone who came near him.

Deep inside, the man longed to be free from the repulsive demons. No one could do anything for him—until Jesus came on the scene. When Jesus asked the man his name, the demons replied, "Legion," which meant he was possessed by a multitude of evil spirits. Jesus sent the evil spirits out and into a herd of pigs feeding nearby. The pigs were undoubtedly startled by the demons and stampeded headlong over a cliff into the Sea of Galilee.

Luke then describes the man free of the demons sitting at Jesus' feet, clothed, and in his right mind (Luke 8:35). The destruction of the pigs and disappearance of the demons marked the transformation of the lunatic man. One word from Jesus had set him free and restored his sanity.

No matter what trap you find yourself or your children in, be it some kind of addiction such as drugs, alcohol, or pornography, Jesus can change anyone. No matter how much God's image in them has been distorted, Jesus can restore it. Jesus can heal and transform their lives the way he did this man.

Until we built a tall fence, we often had our propane gas cylinders stolen at the Bible School in Argentina where we ministered. After we had several stolen, I would go to the villa (ghetto) and buy the cylinders back. It was easy to find our cylinders because they were quickly recognizable. I would say, *"El dueno ha venido a comprar lo suyo"* (the owner has come to buy back what is his). This is what Jesus did for us when he went to the cross. His death can atone for all our sins and give us back our God-given purpose in life. Jesus corrects the distortion that sin has caused in our lives.

Not quitting and not giving up on your family is not always easy because being a responsive parent is hard work. Sometimes it can seem like a thankless job, but if we hang in there, the rewards will come. Your children will respect and love you, and you will reap the joys of your hard work by having a loving family.

Overcoming Your Weaknesses

In the book *The Great Divorce*, which is a fictional book about heaven, C. S. Lewis writes about a young man who is constantly plagued by a red lizard that sits on his shoulder. The lizard constantly taunts the young man, thus perpetuating an inner struggle of choosing right and wrong. An angel from God offers to rid the young man of the pesky lizard. The young man is excited at the idea until the angel declares that he will use fire to kill the lizard. He suddenly realizes that it will involve some pain on his part, and there might be some collateral damage from the fire.

He makes a counter-offer to the angel and asks whether it is really necessary to kill the lizard. Killing the lizard sounds so drastic to the young man, and he wonders if it might be possible to better control the lizard another way. The angel emphatically responds, "In this moment are all moments. Either you want the red lizard to live or you do not." The young man must choose whether or not he wants the lizard dead. The lizard is quick to take advantage of the hesitancy of the young man and attempts to persuade him to let him live.[1] The lizard very carefully talks to the young man:

> Is this something you really want to do? You give in to the angel, and I will be gone forever. The angel is always so dramatic! It's not just yes or no like he says it is. I don't really think you want me gone anyway because I have done so much for you. I have given you pleasure and enjoyment, and I can keep on doing it, but you have to choose to keep me in your life.[2]

Lewis nailed it in this story because that young man is any of us and all of us, and that conversation with the red lizard is the same conversation we have with our own sinful natures. It's what we say when we talk to ourselves. We reason, we rationalize, "Just this time. It won't hurt anyone, after all it's my happiness that matters the most." In the same way, we refuse to deal with the issues that destroy our marriages and devastate our families. Our only hope is to seriously face the problems on the inside and admit we need God's help. This is what it means to not quit. Even if you get counseling, it can be tough because you still have to let God kill the red lizard.

The way C. S. Lewis ends the story about the young man and the lizard is brilliant. The young man finally consents to have the angel kill the lizard. The powerful angel proceeds to crush the lizard in his forceful grip and throw the creature to the ground. Then the young man, as a result of his surrender of the lizard, is transformed into a stronger, more powerful man.

At the same time, the lizard suddenly is changed into a powerful stallion. The young man mounts the beautiful horse and rides him with ease. Lewis says,

The Master says to our master, Come up. Share my rest and splendor till all natures that were your enemies become slaves to dance before you and backs for you to ride, and firmness for your feet to rest on.[3]

When you are finally willing to face the skeletons in your closets and be completely honest with your spouse and your family, you can overcome. What has mastered you and defeated you can be conquered with God's help. However, you have to be willing to persevere and never quit, no matter how hard it gets.

12

Attitude Is Everything

A guy joins a monastery and takes a vow of silence but is allowed to say two words every seven years. After the first seven years, the elders bring him in and ask for his two words. "Cold floors," he says. They nod and send him away. Seven more years pass. They bring him back in and ask for his two words. He clears his throat and says, "Bad food." They nod and send him away. Seven more years pass. They bring him in for his two words. "I quit," he says. "That's not surprising," the elders say. "You've done nothing but complain ever since you got here."

Despite that humorous story, it is impossible to stress how important attitude is in life. It is our compass that points out our direction in life. It is our altimeter that measures our level of functioning. It is our motor that drives our values and beliefs. Unless our attitude is attached to something immovable, such as our belief in God and his Word, our attitude will fluctuate in reaction to day-to-day events. If we have been hurt, and we will be, our attitude will often reflect resentment, bitterness, and even hatred. When this happens, we need healing—healing that comes from forgiveness. In the last chapter I focused on perseverance, and certainly that is an important part of our attitude, but there is much more.

Thanks to neuroscientists such as Daniel Amen, Marian Diamond, Caroline Leaf, and many more, we now know so much more about the brain. We know that love, affirmation, and positive home environment can build a better and stronger emotional intelligence for our children. We also know that a negative environment where there is anxiety and stress will inhibit and impede the growth of a child's brain power. We also know that in adults the presence of strong negative emotion can have a devastating effect on their brain.[1]

Parents do a lot of complaining. We complain about the kids, our spouse, the house, the dog, and on and on. It all comes down to one little word—attitude. Attitude is everything when it comes to parenting. Your attitude as the parent sets the tone for the children. If you are irritable and hard to get along with, they will follow your example. The older child will treat the younger in the same way you are treating him. On the other hand, if you have a persevering attitude that is encouraging, they will model that.

We need to help our children develop a healthy attitude toward themselves and others, and toward God. This assignment can't be delegated. They need you, Mom and Dad, to open up and share your thoughts and experiences. Years later they will reflect back on your conversations with delight.

Appreciating Silence

We live in a world that doesn't appreciate silence. There is noise everywhere you go. If you go to the grocery store, there is music, or in the mall you will be serenaded by some tune. People listen to the radio in their cars or to some kind of device when they are walking or running. Most of us don't know what to do with silence. There are moments, however, when words are inadequate, and any kind of music or noise would be inappropriate.

Such a moment came for Peter when he was on the mountain and he witnessed Jesus' glory revealed. It was as if the spiritual curtain were drawn back and Jesus' glory shown forth. His glorified body radiated through his clothing, and Matthew says, "His face shown like the sun" (17:2). It was only a small glimpse of Jesus' glory before Bethlehem and a peak into what his future glory would be like, but what a glimpse it was! Peter later wrote about what he saw that day, and he never forgot it (1 Pet. 1:7).

At one point Moses and Elijah also appeared in splendor and talked with Jesus about his impending death and resurrection. Though both men had been gone from the earth for nearly 1000 years, there they were before Peter's eyes, talking with Jesus. Peter hardly knew how to contain himself, so he said to Jesus, "Master, it is good for us to be here. Let us put up three shelters—one for you, one for Moses, and one for Elijah" (Luke 9:33). Luke adds that Peter really didn't know what he was saying. Jesus never answered Peter, and I'm sure Peter realized this was a moment that would have been better without any words. It was a moment to stop and contemplate what he was experiencing and not comment on it.

I think there are moments that are sacred, and they don't need any comment. What we really need is to be quiet and take in as much as we can, especially when it comes to God. Many years later Peter did some thinking about what he experienced that day, and he begins by saying that he, John, and James were eyewitnesses of Jesus' majesty:

For he received honor and glory from God the Father when the voice came to him from the Majestic Glory, saying, "This is my Son, whom I love; with him I am well pleased." We ourselves heard this voice that came from heaven when we were with him on the sacred mountain" (2 Pet. 1:16-18).

Sitting in contemplation of who Jesus is, we realize that he is the bread of life, the living water, the light, the way, and the truth. He is the rest we long for and the peace we search for. Sitting in quietness and letting the awe of God's presence overwhelm us often leaves us speechless but strengthens us with a renewed focus for the right things.

Loneliness

Loneliness can be a very devastating force in our lives. It can cause us to doubt God's promises. The prophet Jeremiah knew loneliness. We can see the prophet sitting on the ground with his head buried in his hands. Tears flow freely as Jeremiah vents his innermost feelings. Here Jeremiah records feelings of loneliness, anger, frustration, failure, dejection, and despair. It doesn't get any more real than this.

> *Alas, my mother, that you gave me birth, a man with whom the whole land strives and contends! I have neither lent nor borrowed, yet everyone curses me* (Jer. 15:10).

That's pretty bad, isn't it? It gets worse:

> *I never sat in the company of revelers, never made merry with them; I sat alone because your hand was on me and you had filled me with indignation. Why is my pain unending and my wound grievous and incurable? Will you be to me like a deceptive brook, like a spring that fails?* (Jer. 15:17-18).

Jeremiah wants to know where God is in the midst of his turmoil and strife. He has been obedient to God and has repeatedly delivered the messages from God to the people. Incidentally, all parents experience times like these when you are trying to be the best parent you know to be, but things just don't seem to be working out. You will at times feel your own children's rejection.

Jeremiah felt that even God had rejected him. It seemed to Jeremiah that his prayers were having no effect on God, and he felt all alone and even abandoned by God. His words seemed only to echo off the walls. What was the reason God never answered? Was he too busy? Did he not care? Would he never respond? Where was God when Jeremiah needed him? Jeremiah was dealing with loneliness.

Jeremiah recorded his confession of his struggle with his faith. He said, "I sat alone." We sometimes think of the biblical characters such as Jeremiah as having been great men of faith who never swerved to the right or the left. Jeremiah in his honesty allows us to see a great man in a weak moment. The prophet didn't always feel the presence of God in his life. His walk of faith took him right through the middle of horrific storms, which made him feel as though he were being swept away from his foundation. When he reached out to God for help, he felt he found no one home, so he questioned, "Where are you, God?" Therefore, Jeremiah cried, "I sat alone."

We can relate to Jeremiah because we find when we're in the middle of a storm and overwhelmed with these feelings the prophet dealt with, we often feel abandoned. There are moments like these in all our lives. How important it is to teach the lives of these great men and women of scripture to our children. Let them see the real struggles these heroes faced and how their faith helped them overcome.

Jeremiah believes that God was well aware of what he was going through. The prophet wanted action. "Do something, God!" Does that sound familiar to anyone? He wanted those who were persecuting him to be restrained. He was being mistreated because he was God's prophet. The reaction against the prophet was really against God. Therefore he could say, "O Lord, you are surely aware of what is going on here." In reality this was God's fault. The problem for Jeremiah was that he was doing right and God seemed to be ignoring him. If God would just talk to him, Jeremiah would feel better.

Jeremiah raises a question for which he has no answer.

Why is my pain unending and my wound grievous and incurable? Will you be to me like a deceptive brook, like a spring that fails? (Jer. 15:18).

The prophet asks why his problems never go away. Then he expresses a complaint against God for abandoning him. There are times when he feels God's presence so strongly that it could be compared to a river so large that it would be impossible to cross. Now, however, he feels the river has vanished and dried up, and God has abandoned his servant. The brook is deceptive because it cannot be depended upon for water. Haven't we all felt this way at times?

Loneness

God wanted Jeremiah to turn his loneliness into loneness. What I call loneness is simply being alone with ourselves and God. It is using our solitary time to reflect and not fall into self-pity. We need to learn the difference and how to turn loneliness to loneness. In times of loneness we can hear God's voice and find our way out of the maze of despair. Loneness means that with God's help, we turn a lonely, even discouraging time into a meaningful one of seeing from God's perspective.

God gives Jeremiah not what he asked for but what he needed. His answer to Jeremiah is in the form of a rebuke.

Therefore this is what the LORD says: "If you repent, I will re-store you that you may serve me; if you utter worthy, not worthless, words, you will be my spokesman" (Jer. 15:19).

Let this people turn to you, but you must not turn to them. Jeremiah had often called on the people to repent and return to God, but now it is God who asks Jeremiah to repent of his wrong attitude and return to God.

God tells him that if he turns from worthless talk, he will turn to him and restore him to his prophetic office. The bitterness that had engulfed the prophet had almost silenced his prophetic voice. Those feelings of loneliness had almost caused him to lose sight of God.

Jeremiah knew he had to keep trusting God; maybe others could afford the risk of flinging their faith to the wind but not Jeremiah. Jeremiah did repent and change his attitude, and that is why God's hand remained on him.

Jeremiah had to separate the precious from the worthless and speak words that had value if he were to be God's spokesman. God wanted the prophet not to worry about the people. His only concern should be to obey God and carry the divine message to the people. What a lesson for our kids!

Today the kids hear so many worthless messages growing up that it takes the combined efforts of committed parents to cut them away. They are told they are the victim instead of learning personal responsibility. They are informed that the problems in their lives are somebody else's fault; and if they were smart, good looking, and outgoing, life would be so much more fun. They are told they need more things to be happy, and on and on the lies come. We must be vigilant in watching and listening to our children's attitudes and words so we help them sort the worthless ideas from the valuable ones. God helped Jeremiah prioritize his values, and this is what every parent needs to do to be effective.

Doing the Right Thing

Attitude is about doing the right thing all the time even when you don't feel like it. The story told by Elmer Bendiner in his book, *The Fall of Fortresses,* illustrates that even small things can make a big difference. Elmer shares the account of a B-17 on a bombing mission over Germany during World War II. The plane took a direct hit on their gas tanks.

He wrote, "Our B-17 was barraged by flak from Nazi antiaircraft guns. That was not unusual, but on this particular occasion our gas tanks were hit." Twenty millimeter shells hit the fuel tank without touching off an explosion. Later, the crew chief found eleven shells in the gas tanks, which the crew considered to be a miracle since only one would have been sufficient to blast them out of the sky. The shells were empty and contained no explosive charge, making them completely harmless. However, one of them contained a carefully rolled piece of paper. On it was a note scrawled in Czech that read: "This is all we can do for you now." Random shells empty of explosive material were regularly included in that munitions factory by a brave band of fighters. They were doing what they could do without even knowing the result. That little thing made all the difference in the world for the crew of that B-17.

The same will be true for every parent who does the right thing for their family, which at the time may seem like a thankless job. Your children may not realize your effort and sacrifice until they have their own children. Doing the right thing will make a difference, and sometimes it makes all the difference.[2]

Having the right attitude means that you learn how to talk to your wife or husband with respect. So often couples bring to their relationship learned habits that are disrespectful and hurtful to each other and certainly to the children watching. Determining that you and your spouse are always going to communicate in a respectful way comes down to controlling your own attitude. You will mess up and make mistakes, but most of the time you will do it right, and that makes life enjoyable. It makes you want to come home and enjoy your wife or husband and be with your family.

Taking Responsibility

Facing problems squarely and not running from them is called taking responsibility, the mark of true leadership. Life is made up of a series of problems, and raising strong, emotionally healthy children depends on our willingness to tackle the problems with courage. Avoiding problems, blaming them on other people, and pretending they don't exist will only make them worse. The sooner we face our problems and deal with them, the greater our quality of life. Sometimes parents run from problems with their toddler because they seem overwhelming, but they only get more complicated the longer we procrastinate. Other parents ignore obvious problems with their teenagers, but the problems only get bigger and scarier when ignored. Being a problem solver isn't easy, but it's easier than ignoring the problems. As a bonus, parents who take responsibility for their problems also teach their children to do the same.

How we live is how we die. If a person has been a complainer during their childhood, young adulthood, and middle ages, they will be that way in the last part of their life. However, it will be worse because problems are greater when health and strength are diminished. It's a sad thing to see a person in their 70s and 80s who is cranky and grouchy. What we don't always realize is that they were always that way, but now they are so much worse. You want to leave your children and grandchildren a legacy of wisdom, integrity, faithfulness, and gratitude, not one of a complaining, bad-tempered old man or woman. You can choose your attitude; you are not a victim of circumstance. Choose to live with a great attitude and pass it on to your children as part of your legacy.

13

Overcoming Adversity

My father owned a trucking business, so I learned to drive big trucks when I was a young man. When you are learning a new skill, you make a few mistakes no matter what your endeavor. I can remember taking out a few fence posts and backing into a water tank while learning how to maneuver a 40-foot semi. Those mistakes, however, made me a better driver. I never turned into a narrow place again without remembering the mistake of hitting that fence.

Parenting is no different for the conscientious parent who wants to learn. Learning from our mistakes is one of the best ways to learn. The only people who have all the answers for parents are the ones who don't have any kids. My, how well these people would do the job if they had kids! Those of us who have been parents know it's not easy—you just have to learn some things on the job. You can't know all you need to know when the little ones first arrive. However, being willing to learn is of the utmost importance, and learning from your mistakes is a great way to begin.

You may recognize that you have been too hard or too easy as a parent, but being willing to make an adjustment is really important. Responsive parenting is all about parenting your child in such a way that he or she develops a capacity to manage life successfully without you.

Often young parents choose making their child happy as the goal of parenting. This kind of parenting can be an overwhelming task, especially when your child realizes that this is your goal. The "trying to make your child happy" parenting style creates dependence and diminishes autonomy in the child. Secondly, it's not real life because when your child is old enough to go to school or be around other people, she will discover things are very different. The teacher cannot see her principle task as trying to make your child happy. Of course, we all want our children to be happy, but happiness has to come as a result of other things not because it is our primary pursuit in life.

To Build Integrity, Get Started Early

I ran across a poem many years ago entitled, "Just a Nobody," written in Spanish by Aracely Maldonado. The piece begins with the devastating news that the author is HIV positive. In a tone of regret and reflection the writer asks:

What is a harvest? I don't even know what a good plant is, a quality fruit, or for that matter even a decent seed. This is not what I thought life was supposed to be—there has to be more. I thought life was meant to go somewhere. What of my dreams? There was a day I really believed they were true. Then things got all mixed up—-only a few days ago someone with a white coat told me I was HIV positive. From that moment everything changed, the atmosphere seemed different—with obliged smiles and hypocritical faces that tell you they understand. What do they understand? Do they comprehend that your energy is gone and along with it, all your dreams have vanished? Do they have any idea of how upside down your life has become or what a terrible destiny you now face?

Then it dawns on you that this is life. You're nobody. Life is like a giant chess game and you're not a king or queen— you're nothing but a pawn. What of the harvest? Then I remember that to plant, you need a seed, but what if the seed is bad, what if it's worthless? What if it never even existed?[1]

You can feel the author's disappointment. He doesn't like the way things have turned out. He feels he never even had a choice because things were bad from the start. He resents being the victim and being powerless to change anything.

This poem could have been written by Joseph in the first book of the Bible, Genesis. Nowhere in the Bible does any life take more wrong turns than in the life of Joseph. If anyone could have taken a pessimistic view of life, it should have been him. No doubt he knew what it felt like to be a pawn in life's game of chess; he would, however, have written a different ending to the poem. Despite the fact that Joseph was betrayed and humiliated, he finished well. He wasn't overcome by his trouble; instead, he overcame his trouble. His story is one of the most inspiring in the Bible.

Don Anderson comments on Joseph's life:

Joseph is not bound by his circumstances. He is wrapped up in his God. He is content, submissive, and obedient to the father's wishes, completely convinced that the Lord has ordered his situation."[2]

Joseph's story is not some isolated story in the Bible, rather it is every person's story who is willing to travel through life with God.

If you admire Joseph and would like your son or daughter to turn out like him, then here is your challenge: Start now! Start early! Sow the good seeds generously and cultivate a harvest of character in your child. Joseph didn't develop character in adversity, but his character was revealed in his adversity. What you teach your child will help her face life head on or become a victim.

It is not *if* bad things will happen to us, but *when* bad things will happen. From time to time, people will hurt our children with their words and cruel actions. We can't always protect our children from getting hurt, but we can prepare them to respond in the right way. Unfortunate circumstances beyond our control will occur, but we can prepare our children for the unexpected by teaching them to trust God in every situation. Then they will learn to respond in the right way.

First, Joseph survived because someone planted in him the good seeds of God's word. Introduce your children to God as soon as they are old enough to comprehend. If your faith is authentic, your children will buy into your values and beliefs. If your faith is real and it works in your life and in the family, your kids will find it attractive.

Secondly, Joseph overcame his impossible situation because he had uncompromising integrity. Teach your child the difference between right and wrong. Set the boundaries of good behavior and give your child a home filled with love that is marked by discipline. We are seeing young people today who don't know how to think logically and who have no moral compass. These important tools can be given very early in life by responsible parents.

Thirdly, he triumphed because he learned to trust God in impossible situations. Teach your child who God is—that He is a God of love, mercy and justice. Teach him that God will never abandon him, but he will have to learn to wait on God. In doing these things, you will build the foundation for a life of integrity in your child.

Turning Setbacks Into Milestones

When Joseph was only seventeen, he had a sense of what was right and wrong. He had a sense of purpose, and he had dreams of greatness. Joseph was not raised in a perfect home—far from it. Jacob, his father, showed him favoritism, which is a terrible mistake parents can make. Jacob's unfairness contributed to the brothers' negative attitudes toward Joseph. When Joseph told his dreams to his brothers, they hated him even more.

Parents, you don't have to be a perfect parent to raise a Joseph. Jacob was flawed—but he was for real. He loved God and tried to live a sincere life of faith. Jacob's life radically turned around after his older sons were grown men. His early example for them was much less sincere because the old Jacob was a schemer. Jacob had been a heel-grabber his whole life, but God had slowly transformed him into a God-seeker. Most importantly, though, Jacob had learned from his own mistakes.

The impact of your life on your sons and daughters is immeasurable. Never be discouraged by your mistakes or shortfalls; just start today with what you now have and do your best. Do not be afraid to talk about your mistakes with your children. They will respect you and learn from you as a result. It's not how bad your mistakes were, but how much you've changed since you made them.

If you ask God for his help, you will receive it. Take heart in the parenting skills of Jacob. If he was able to raise a Joseph, you can too. In fact, eventually even the older sons changed by the grace of God. Jacob faced some impossible situations in his life, and most of them were self-inflicted. He learned, however, that if he would humble himself and ask forgiveness, God can change people and circumstances.

Remember that even though the bad choices of others may negatively impact us, God can overrule them if we are committed to him. Our right choices will trump their bad choices. How comforting to think that we are never at the mercy of others when we know and trust God. The bad intentions of others cannot frustrate God's purposes in our lives. King Nebuchadnezzar of Babylon learned that and stated it in his testimony:

> *All the peoples of the earth are regarded as nothing. He does as he pleases with the powers of heaven and the peoples of the earth. No one can hold back his hand or say to him: "What have you done?"* (Daniel 4:35)

Joseph was sent to check on his brothers who were tending the flocks. When the brothers saw Joseph coming, they came up with a scheme of how they would kill him. They decided to throw him into a dry cistern and let him die (Gen. 37:19-20). The brothers' hatred had driven them to the point of no return—they were ready for murder. As the unsuspecting teenager approached his brothers, he had no idea he was walking into a trap.

Eventually the brothers wound up selling Joseph as a slave. They showed Joseph's coat covered in goat blood to their father, telling him they had found it, and asked him whether it was Joseph's. They heartlessly watched their father come to the desired conclusion as he recognized the coat and exclaimed, "It is my son's robe" (Gen. 37:33).

These deceitful men had a propensity toward evil. The brothers would look back with regret on their deed, but on this day they were under the spell of the mob. That was a terrible thing to do to Joseph and to their father, but no evil can stop God from working his plans out. No matter what tragedies have happened in your family, turn to God and let him begin his work.

Joseph was taken to Egypt and sold to Potiphar. This could have been the end of the story for Joseph had he not been a young man of character. This story is not about the tragedy done against Joseph, rather it is about the marvelous way God takes whatever happens to us and works it out according to what he wants. God is in charge and no one can change that. You may not be where you want to be, nor doing what you want to do; however, it doesn't matter if you are fully committed to God.

When your children feel cheated, you can indulge their self-pity and enable them to feel victimized, or you can acknowledge the hurt as real and encourage them to turn it over to God. Pray with them and believe that God will work through their circumstances. Help them develop skills that prepare them to deal with unpleasant and unexpected circumstances.

Joseph's presence made a difference to the household of Potiphar, "The blessing of the Lord was on everything Potiphar had" (Gen. 39:5). This wasn't magic; it was God. God's hand was upon Joseph. He had no clout or influence, yet in spite of this, Joseph was promoted to manage Potiphar's household.

Joseph refused to be dominated by his culture. His character became more and more defined to those who knew him and serves as a model for all of us. He was surrounded by temptations and pitfalls, but he never stopped doing what was right.

He sought to do his best, and his life reflected his integrity and commitment to God. Doing right didn't always give him an advantage, but he kept his head and stayed the course.

The prophet Habakkuk stated this principle of faithfulness in some of the most eloquent words ever written:

> *Though the fig tree does not bud and there are no grapes on the vines, though the olive crop fails and the fields produce no food, though there are no sheep in the pen and no cattle in the stalls, yet I will rejoice in the LORD, I will be joyful in God my Savior. The Sovereign LORD is my strength* (Hab. 3:17-19).

Joseph remained faithful even though there were no grapes on the vine and no sheep in the pens.

Letting Go of Our Hurts

Character insists on being patient in the face of affliction. Joseph determined to keep his faith in God even if he was all alone. He did his best because he had the right kind of attitude. The fact that the Lord was with Joseph and gave him success at everything he did was not an accident; rather, it was because of God's blessings on Joseph's life. God was not a genie in a bottle to Joseph, giving him every whim and fancy, but He blessed Joseph's faithfulness.

Several years later, Joseph named his first son Manasseh, which meant, "It is because God has made me forget all my trouble and all my father's household," (Gen. 41:51). In later years, Joseph looked back with gratitude and said that the only reason he survived that entire ordeal was because God helped him to forget.

It is truly amazing that God enabled Joseph to forgive the cruelty that had been dealt him. Consequently, Joseph experienced freedom when he forgave his brothers and the others who had betrayed him. How important it is for us to let the hurts go! If we don't, they are like an infection is to the body and do immeasurable harm to us and to those around us. Joseph never really forgot what happened to him, but what he did do was refuse the resentment, bitterness, and hate that wanted to fill his heart. Only God can help you do that.

Some people, still after many years, resent the place where they are in life. Some dream about a different life than the one they have. Some hate their jobs and can't seem to put their whole heart into their work. No one will flourish in life until they accept their station in life and forgive those who have hurt them.

Later, Joseph named his second son Ephraim, which meant, "It is because God has made me fruitful in the land of my suffering" (Gen. 41:52). He knew the reason things were going well. He knew that God was making him bloom where he was planted. It was evident to Potiphar that his household and business were prospering because of Joseph, and so he promoted him to be in charge of everything.

Character Revealed in the Trial

Potiphar was confident that his estate was being managed wisely with Joseph in charge. However, the next attack that came against Joseph did not have to do with his management skills but was an attack against his character. Joseph was a handsome man, and his boss' wife tried to seduce him, "But he refused" (Gen. 39:6).

To refuse meant saying no to a tempting moment of pleasure that had a powerful lure over Joseph. It meant saying no to an illicit affair. It meant saying no to temptation that would have soiled Joseph's character and stolen God's blessings from his life.

Joseph declined the temptation because of his loyalty to his boss. Secondly, Joseph questioned how he could do such a wicked thing against God. Even though the woman tried to have her way with Joseph day after day, he continually refused. Joseph was prepared for these moments by his convictions.

I love the inspiring story of Joseph's life. There are a few things that stand out to me such as his ability to forgive people who hurt him, his persevering attitude in the face of disappointing setbacks, and his ability to rule over his own desires. Joseph had the ability to control himself in very difficult situations. We hear today that kind of self-control should not be expected from young people. People say that too many extenuating circumstances mitigate a young person's ability to control themselves, such as poverty, a dysfunctional home, or growing up as part of a minority.

Joseph demonstrated how a young man or young woman can have self-control. He was set up by his master's wife. She cornered him when he was alone and there was no one else around. When she said to him, "Come to bed with me," Joseph refused (Gen. 39:7-12). Joseph gave her his reasons of loyalty and integrity. When young people are raised with a sense of integrity and morality, they can say no to temptation. Those two qualities produce inner strength that helps them rule over their spirit. They are not a slave to their passions and helpless to the demands of their sexual hormones. Joseph demonstrated that a young person can say no to seductive temptations that would ruin their lives so they can later say yes to the one right person, which Joseph did when he later married, had two sons, and enjoyed his family.

God made sex for marriage, and within those confines it meets the emotional and physical needs of the couple. Sex outside that bond will never be completely satisfying—it will always demand more.

I remember watching Dr. James Dobson's interview with Ted Bundy, the infamous serial killer, just before he was executed. Bundy's own admission was that he got started on pornography very early and could never be satisfied with any real sexual encounter. His desires controlled him and always demanded more until eventually he became a killer.

Not every person involved in pornography becomes a killer, but they will experience that same unfulfilled desire. They will be more controlled by their desires and less connected to real, meaningful relationships. Joseph is a picture of what God intended for all of us. Today the lies are everywhere that it doesn't matter if you live with someone or become sexually active before marriage. I deal everyday with broken lives that would say otherwise.

Once Potiphar heard the story, Joseph was put in prison. Joseph was in prison for doing right, so how is that fair? It may not have been fair, but Joseph looked back on that day with gratitude that God was with him. For thirteen years Joseph served God in faithfulness and integrity even though it looked as if he would never really be vindicated.

Then one routine day, soldiers arrived to escort Joseph to the presence of Pharaoh. Within a few hours he was promoted from keeper of the prison to Prime Minister of the most powerful nation on the face of the earth. Joseph had refused Satan's offer to compromise his convictions and chose to rely on God's faithfulness. It was God behind Pharaoh's offer to Joseph. It will also be God behind the circumstances that will one day come knocking on your door if you remain faithful to God. How important to teach this to our children! We do so by planting good seeds each day. Water and cultivate your children, and one day you will see a man or woman of character, and you will be so grateful.

14

⟨∼⟩

Learning Self-Control

The older I get, the more I realize that self-control is so important in life and is essential to being good at anything we do. Just think about how great athletes have to perfect self-control in their handling of the ball, the bat, or whatever their sport requires. Self-control is about mastering concentration and staying focused. However, the greatest self-control is needed when it comes to interpersonal relationships. If you want to be a good husband or wife or great parent, you have to learn to exercise self-control.

Self-control is the area that is most difficult to master. It is ourselves—our anger, our feelings of rejection, and a host of negative emotions—that is difficult to master. The superstar athlete may be fantastic on the field but a complete disaster at home. No challenge in human existence can be more difficult than the exercising of control over our emotions, which translates into words and actions when we are confronted with opposing emotions. Living with those we love may be the most challenging arena in which to do battle with those emotions.

Jesus showed so us how to live with self-restraint. The New Testament writers highlight this characteristic about Jesus. The following is one of the most remarkable statements about Jesus in the whole of the Bible that was made within a setting of rejection. Matthew includes this quote from Isaiah to underscore

Jesus' self-control when he was being rejected by the Jewish leaders. Rejection is one of the most difficult human emotions to deal with, but Jesus overcame any tendency to give in to it. Matthew states:

> *But the Pharisees went out and plotted how they might kill Jesus. Aware of this, Jesus withdrew from that place. Many followed him, and he healed all their sick, warning them not to tell who he was* (Matt. 12:14-16).

Jesus used incredible self-control and restraint even though he was rejected. He could simply have told his followers what the Pharisees were planning, but he didn't. He could have been so discouraged that he stopped ministering to people, but he didn't. He could have let everyone know who he was and demanded his way, but he didn't. He lived under the control of self-restraint.

The following are Isaiah's words about Jesus written 700 years before Jesus fulfilled them:

> *He will not quarrel or cry out; no one will hear his voice in the streets. A bruised reed he will not break, and a smoldering wick he will not snuff out, till he leads justice to victory. In his name the nations will put their hope* (Matt. 12:19-21).

What a commentary on Jesus' ability to control himself and stay on mission, no matter what was happening around him!

Marriages would improve immediately, parenting would be transformed, teamwork on the job would advance, and a sense of community would grow in our congregations when we learn to exercise more self-control. It would mean we listen more and talk less; and when we do talk, we have something to say. When we apologize, we actually explain what we did and how we plan to change our attitude and behavior. Self-control gives us insight into our own lives and those around us like nothing else can do. Jesus lived in this way, and we, his followers, are to live like him.

Let's look at self-control in the following fictitious story about two different couples. One uses self-control in a difficult situation, and the other is controlled by their emotions. Couple A gets up on a leisurely Saturday morning and is enjoying their time together, when out of nowhere a ferocious argument begins. The arguing is so great that the man storms out of the house without saying where he is going or when he is coming back, leaving the wife crying.

Couple B starts out their Saturday in much the same way with the same argument. However, when things get so hot this man says he is leaving, he also states where he is going, when he is coming back, and that he would like to talk when he returns. The wife, though very upset, agrees. A few hours later, the first man comes back and acts as if nothing ever happened, and so does his wife. It's their way of dealing with a severe conflict.

When the second man returns, however, he and his wife have lunch and talk about what had happened. Each reflects on what they each did, and together they come to a resolution and thereby learn from what happened. The difference between the two couples is self-control, and it contributes to the quality of the relationship and the home.

In 1999, John Gottman and Nan Silver wrote a book entitled, *The Seven Principles for Making Marriage Work*. Gottman named four horsemen that destroy marriage: criticism, contempt, defensiveness, and stonewalling.[1] Gottman was right because when these devastating patterns take hold of a marriage, it will crumble. Not only will the marriage not survive, the destructive patterns will be passed on to the children. How do these patterns get started and how are they perpetuated? It is because of a lack of self-control. Old habits are hard to break, and new healthy patterns can only be initiated with enormous effort and self-restraint.

Breaking Old Habits

My father-in-law was a chicken farmer. He would receive 50,000 baby chicks in two giant truckloads, and it would take a few days to get everything situated. I watched him many times pull a chick from the enclosure. "Why did you take that chick out?" I would ask. "It's different—see the specks on it; and because it's different, the other chicks will peck it to death."

I have observed that chicks are not the only creatures that do that. Humans also have a way of attacking other humans who are different. In Jesus' Sermon on the Mount, he taught us to have an accepting spirit.

Do not judge, and you will not be judged. Do not condemn, and you will not be condemned. Forgive, and you will be forgiven (Luke 6:37).

This is one of the most misunderstood verses in the Bible. People love to quote this verse out of context because judging is thought to be such a politically incorrect thing. Jesus, however, is not referring to making moral judgments because verses 43-45 make that clear where he talks about judging a person by their fruit. Jesus is talking about our being petty and going around with a critical spirit. Nothing is more miserable than to be around a know-it-all who can see what is wrong with everyone but himself. Jesus, in effect, is saying, "Stop being suspicious of everyone. Stop finding fault with people around you.

Stop focusing on the failings of others." To do so is hypocritical if you haven't dealt with your own failings first. Jesus said, "Why do you look at the speck of sawdust in your brother's eye and pay no attention to the plank in your own eye?" (Luke 6:41)

Jesus' illustration is so extreme because he wants us to see our need to deal with our problems first before trying to help someone else. Jesus continues,

> *How can you say to your brother, "Brother, let me take the speck out of your eye," when you yourself fail to see the plank in your own eye? You hypocrite, first take the plank out of your eye, and then you will see clearly to remove the speck from your brother's eye* (Luke 6:42)

Before we can try to help anyone with their speck, we have to deal with our own failings. It's the height of hypocrisy to strut around inspecting eyeballs for specks while we have a plank hanging out of our own eye. Only when we have removed the plank from our eye can we see clearly to help our brother in a spirit of compassion and mercy. Then we seek to restore them because we understand what it is all about since God has showed us mercy. Only when we have dealt with the log hanging out of our eye can we really begin to be the parent we want to be. Jesus' illustration is really the formula for good parenting. We need to deal with our irritating and embarrassing problems before dealing with our children's issues.

The Apostle Paul said that love is not irritable (1 Cor. 13:5), which is quite a statement when you think about it. How many of us could say that we love without being irritated at those we live with? Very likely most of us would come up short. All of us know something about irritability. It's what we do when we are frustrated and is mostly in response to little things. It might be the way someone talks or doesn't talk to us, the way they eat, or a hundred other things. I would like to suggest that our irritability is our inability to control our emotions.

Most tend to blame others for their irritability, saying things like, "He knows just how to push my buttons" or "She makes me so frustrated." I can't even begin to tell you how many times I have heard those words in counseling sessions from both husbands and wives. The primary issue according to Paul is not how irritating the other person is, but how willing I am to be responsible for my own attitude.

Often we find ourselves very irritated by another's actions because we have allowed our emotions to run rampant. Instead of thinking through what is happening to us and asking God to help us, more often than not we give in to the irritation. When our emotions are controlling us, we aren't doing too much thinking, which is a dangerous place to be. When we are irritated, we are vulnerable to outbursts of anger. Of course, when we are angry we say things we really don't mean, harming those around us. Augustine wrote, "We are irritable, O Lord, until we make our peace with you."[2]

I think Augustine was right. The key to controlling our emotions is to trust God with our inabilities and allow him to teach us how to handle life's frustrations. When our relationship with God is connected and alive, we have inner strength to control our emotions. We are more in control because we are anchored to the One who gives us peace. Anger and frustration may seem uncontrollable, but they are with God's help.

Our Worst Fears

Fear is a paralyzing thing, freezing our response to something frightening, or causing us to either run away or fight. Fear actually cripples us in so many ways. Take, for example, someone who fears not being accepted. The fear of rejection is one of the most common fears known to humanity. It is an enslaving fear because it controls how we think and act.

The fear of failing is also a powerful force that can fetter us in so many different ways. Often we will not attempt something we would really like to do because we are afraid of the possibility of failure. The fear of not having enough feeds our scarcity mentality, and this mentality makes us to be stingy and petty. It is completely miserable to be raised by a petty father. There are also fears of not having the ideal body, the fear of losing our health, the fear of harm, and on and on the list goes.

Zachariah, the father of John the Baptist, sang about Jesus' ministry before he was born in Bethlehem. He said that Jesus would "rescue us from the hand of our enemies, and...enable us to serve him without fear" (Luke 1:74). We need to be rescued from our fears and delivered from them to be able to live our lives with purpose and meaning. Jesus can do that for us. Instead of living in depression or overwhelmed by anxiety—confined by fear—Jesus will set us free and enable us to serve.

Once we have been delivered from fear, we can use our gifts and talents for his glory in creative ways that benefit others. Being set free from our fears enables us to be a better husband, wife, and parent. Most parents have fears about whether or not they are doing a good job and how their children will turn out. Fear is a paralyzing thing that hinders our performance as parents. Being delivered from fear frees you to be who you really want to be.

Dr. John Gottman believes every child has the fear of abandonment.[3] Many of the well-known children's stories revolve around this theme. We should never threaten or even joke about this fear because it is so real. Not understanding a child's fears and not respecting the emotion of fear will only heighten the fear. It might be the fear of the dark or fear of death—we should understand that it is real, and our understanding is the first comfort we offer our children. Then we find other ways to comfort them through our presence and through our faith. Little by little we help them overcome their fear of abandonment by our unconditional love for them the same way the Lord does for us.

Winning the Battle Over Worry

No doubt about it, our favorite sin is worry. Anxiety is more common to humanity than any of us care to admit. No one is exempt; no money or fame can place you beyond the reach of anxiety. From an early age all of us begin to experience the feelings that create the state of being anxious. Some, of course, more than others because they are raised in homes where conflict is a way of life, and there is very little conflict resolution.

These feelings of anxiety come for a host of different reasons, from things not going our way to our being mistreated, insulted, or neglected. Interestingly, the older we get the more anxiety we are prone to experience. The late Corrie Ten Boom used to say, "Worry does not rob today of its sorrow, but tomorrow of its strength." Anxiety is nothing new because Solomon in the book of Ecclesiastes gives us some good advice on how to lessen our anxiety.

Solomon said, "So then, banish anxiety from your heart and cast off the troubles of your body, for youth and vigor are meaningless" (Eccl. 11:10).

He knows from experience that our broken world brings us

trouble of all kinds and tells us to cast off these troubles. In other words, rather than dwelling on what has happened to us, which usually perpetuates the problem, cast it off. This is done by giving it to God. Many marriages can't progress beyond their past. Each one can't forget the hurt they received from the other. How do we banish anxiety from our life?

The Apostle Peter tells us to: "Cast all your anxiety on him because he cares for you" (1 Pet. 5:7). The very act of casting our anxieties on the Lord means that we are asking for his assistance and trusting him to help us. It means that we are refusing to be tormented any longer by the loss or irritation that has come to us. We acknowledge that "the worry and anxiety is too much for me and I am therefore giving this burden to you, Lord." Most of what we worry about never comes to pass anyway. That is what Jesus said to us in his Sermon on the Mount:

> *Therefore do not worry about tomorrow, for tomorrow will worry about itself. Each day has enough trouble of its own* (Matt. 6:34).

The Apostle Paul actually gave us a spiritual recipe for dealing with anxiety. First, we start by counting our blessings and learning to see the good instead of the loss. Second, we learn to act right regardless of how we feel. Third, we commit to God in prayer all our worries and anxieties. Fourth, as a result of having done that, we receive peace that transforms us to be capable of enjoying life. That peace is a gift from God! And fifth, we train our thinking to stay centered on things that are true and uplifting (Phil. 4: 4-9).

If more people followed this biblical method for peace and sanity, there would be less depression, less people on medication, and a whole lot less sadness in the world. Everyone who casts their anxiety away and trusts God for peace would experience a better quality of life. To not realize that youth is so temporal and fleeting is to not have a grip on reality. Solomon says to enjoy life and not let anxiety rob you of appreciating it. He says that we should not be saddened by the loss of youth because it is only one part of life. Instead, enjoy life because you belong to God at whatever age you find yourself.

Impulsiveness or Thoughtfulness

Impulsiveness, thoughtlessness, carelessness, yelling, screaming, name calling, avoidance behavior, anger, resentment, irritation, anxiety, stressful, and uncontrolled are words that belong to reactive thinking. Words that describe responsive thinking are: deliberate, thoughtful, creative, careful, intelligent, responsible, peaceful, and controlled. These two very opposite ways of dealing with things begin very early in our thinking and continue throughout our lives.

Reactive thinking contributes to dysfunctional behavioral patterns that perpetuate stress and anxiety. On the other hand, responsive thinking contributes to optimum behavioral patterns that promote peaceful and enjoyable relationships. These relationships produce mutual satisfaction. When we are responsive, we create opportunities for better interaction. In other words, we can change our own quality of life by learning how to think right. When we are reactive thinkers, we are our own worst enemy. Whether we are reactive or responsive depends on our level of self-control.

An episode from David's life demonstrates both patterns. While David and his men are in the Desert of Maon, they provide protection for the shepherds of a wealthy man named Nabal. It was not uncommon for attacking tribes to invade and take what they wanted from a herd. This, however, had not happened on David's watch. Since David and his men provided this service, they expected to be recompensed in some way. That's why David sent his men to Nabal for provisions. Nabal's reaction was impulsive and foolish:

> *Who is this David? Who is this son of Jesse? Many servants are breaking away from their masters these days. Why should I take my bread and water, and the meat I have slaughtered for my shearers, and give it to men coming from who knows where?* (1 Sam. 25:9)

David did what most of us do when we are insulted or treated rudely—he got angry. David said to his men, "Put on your swords!" (1 Sam. 25:12). This is the same man who only recently had the chance to kill King Saul but refused to do so. At that point he had demonstrated enormous patience and self-control, even persuading his men of the rightness of his actions. However, now look at David as he is in reactive mode. Alan Redpath writes about this moment with clarity:

> David! David! What is wrong with you? Why, one of the most wonderful things we have learned about you recently is your patience with Saul. You learned to wait upon the Lord, you refused to lift your hand to touch the Lord's anointed, although he had been your enemy for so many years. But now, look at you! Your self-restraint has gone to pieces and a few insulting words from a fool of a man like Nabal has made you see red! David, what's the matter? "I am justified in doing this," David would reply. "There is no reason why Nabal should treat me as he has. He has repaid all my kindness with insults. I will show him he can't trifle

with me. It is one thing to take it from Saul, who is my superior at this point, but this sort of man—this highhanded individual must be taught a lesson!"[4]

However, Abigail, Nabal's wife, is reasonable, self-controlled, and responsive in her thinking. She quickly prepares to go and meet with David before tragedy strikes, taking food and drink as gifts for David's men. She is calm and thoughtful in her actions, completely the opposite of what David is doing.

David is not thinking—he is like a ricocheted bullet bouncing off objects. He is in total reactionary mode and not thinking about his decisions. If David proceeds, he will act in his temporary insanity; and then after all is over, he will come to see what he has done and only then perceive the consequences of his actions. Abigail, however, is able to imagine the consequences before they are enacted and to choose a different course of action. She is a picture of self-control and responsive thinking.

When Abigail encounters David and his men, she doesn't make excuses, instead she accepts responsibility for what has happened and offers to rectify what has been done. She is thoughtful, tactful, courteous, and demonstrates great faith. She accepts the blame for something she had nothing to do with and deliberately takes responsibility for the situation. She says, "If I had talked to those young men you sent, they would have been sent back in a different way. I'm sorry they were dealt with that way." She confidently responds with cogent thoughts and articulate words that change David's mind.

Anger will not subside until someone is willing to accept responsibility for what happened by offering hope that things can be different and is willing to make meaningful apologies.

Dealing with anger is difficult because when we are angry, we really don't see things straight. Abigail shows us it can be done. She regrets what has happened in the past but makes assurances that she will do something about the present, which is what it takes to diffuse the anger in an angry person. Abigail is an example of responsive thinking and acting, and thus self-control.

In all our interpersonal relationships we can be reactive or responsive. It is a choice for each of us. One brings harm and hurt, and the other healing and meaning. Whether it is in marriage, parenting, or workplace relationships, let us strive for responsive thinking and acting. Good marriages, good parenting, and good living begin with self-control and responsive thinking. When things go well and people treat us nicely, we don't need to be responsive. But things don't always go well. Consequently, we need to learn how to think and act under pressure.

Modeling Self-Control

Do you ever find yourself in a place where you wish you could get some good advice? What should I do in this situation, and how should I proceed? Young Timothy, Paul's assistant, found himself in that place as he tried to deal with some very complicated problems in Ephesus. There were some people causing problems, and they needed to be confronted. It was time to bring order out of the chaos.

Paul offered Timothy the following advice:

But you, man of God, flee from all this, and pursue righteousness, godliness, faith, love, endurance and gentleness. Fight the good fight of the faith. Take hold of the eternal life to which you were called when you made your good confession in the presence of many witnesses (1 Tim. 6:11-12).

Paul gave Timothy four commands that can be remembered easily—*flee, pursue, fight,* and *take hold of.* Paul exhorts Timothy to *flee* any situation that had the appearance of evil, whether it was a religious controversy, materialism, or sexual temptation. Flight is sometimes our best option, as it was for Joseph in the book of Genesis when he faced sexual temptation. Fleeing that moment preserved Joseph's character.

Secondly, Paul told Timothy what to *pursue.* He gave him three pairs of pursuits, the first being righteousness and godliness, which is our relationship with God and people. God does one for us, and the other we do for ourselves. Secondly, he told him to pursue faith and love. Without an authentic faith, we will never know God's love. These two virtues are worth our pursuit. Finally, he told him to pursue endurance with gentleness. What contrasting qualities—one is hard as steel and the other soft as cotton, and yet both are needed in our lives. We need to be strong in our convictions yet gentle in our spirit.

Next, Paul commanded Timothy to *fight.* Paul was a fighter, and those who followed him learned to fight the good fight of faith. Timothy was being asked to keep his eye on the prize, which is Jesus Christ, and run hard in the race. "Give it all you have, Timothy." If we want to hang on to our families, we will have to fight for them. Our children and teens will go through stages where they are confused, disappointed, and even angry. We have to help them through these times. We have to step up to the plate and guide them even if a negative emotion is directed toward us as parents. Paul's advice to Timothy is so essential because our example to our children is what is shaping their lives.

One morning I watched a young mother enter our church with both hands loaded with groceries for a special lunch. I opened the door for her and her three-year-old daughter. The mother proceeded down the stairs with ease even though there was considerable oncoming traffic, but the small child chose not to navigate against the flow of people. She stayed put at the top of the stairs with her eyes glued on her mom. The mother walked about twenty feet and suddenly noticed her daughter wasn't at her side, so she turned and spotted her at the top of the stairs. Very gently she spoke to the little girl, "Come on, sweet pea." The three-year-old spoke up and said, "I thought you had lost me." The incident reminded me of how important it is to constantly keep our eyes on our children as they grow up, not just physically but also emotionally and spiritually.

Life presents some challenging moments to our children, and it becomes very difficult for them to go against the current unless they have a model to follow. Sometimes they need to see us stop and turn around and look for them, speaking to them with a concerned voice so they know how much they mean to us.

If we are going to model self-control for our children, we will have to pursue authenticity and be completely real! We have to take responsibility for our actions and our families, and stop making excuses for our failures by doing something about them. If you are still making excuses for why you are not living your life the way you would like—a life that honors God—then you are caught in a web of deceit.

Some people are convinced the reason they have a bad marriage is that they have a bad spouse. Others don't like their work because they have a bad boss. Did you know that God is not into accepting excuses? He doesn't let us get away with our cover-ups. God wants each of us to see the problem right where it lies—inside of each of us.

Crucial Areas Where Self-Control Is Needed

The prophet Isaiah holds up six wild bunches of grapes as a picture of what was wrong with the people of Israel. Each of these areas are the same ones where many families fail. We need to pay attention to what Isaiah is pointing out to us here. Each bunch begins with a "Woe," which is a sad word describing the disappointing grapes. These six things can also be applied to irresponsible parenting going on today.

1. The first is a picture of *how greed destroys us*.

Woe to you who add house to house and join field to field till no space is left and you live alone in the land (Isaiah 5:8).

Human nature hasn't changed one iota. The people sought to get more and better things, living as if God weren't around, and they didn't have any responsibility to their neighbor. Their greed caused them to crave more and never be satisfied. When parents are greedy and irresponsible, they get themselves in debt up to their eyeballs and hurt their family. Their greed places stress on the family and impedes them from reaching their financial goals. Most families in debt don't even have any financial goals. It also gives the children an irresponsible example of how to handle finances.

2. The second bunch shows *how addictions rob us.*

Woe to those who rise early in the morning to run after their drinks, who stay up late at night till they are inflamed with wine. They have harps and lyres at their banquets, tambourines and flutes and wine, but they have no regard for the deeds of the LORD, no respect for the work of his hands (Isaiah 5:11-12).

149

Here the prophet's words are more far reaching than just alcohol; he is merely using alcohol as an illustration. Addictions that control our lives are about our pursuit of pleasure with no regard for God or responsibility. Addictions impede life, and they certainly contribute to bad parenting. It stands to reason if a mom or a dad is addicted to any substance, whether that is alcohol or prescription drugs, they are handicapped. What is frightening is that this problem is so much more widespread than most of us really imagine.

3. The third bunch represents ***the burdens of sin that blind us.***

Woe to those who draw sin along with cords of deceit, and wickedness as with cart ropes (Isaiah 5:18).

What may have once been so clear becomes blurred because of our sin. We carry with us resentment, bitterness, and even hatred. We draw it along behind us from one year to the next. Our sin deceives us and makes us doubt God's love and power. It makes us cynical and unbelieving. Bev Savage tells about seeing a documentary where horses were harnessed to heavy carts and whipped into competing against each other. The horses strained to pull the heavy loads, and some were even destroyed in the process.[5]

How many parents are pulling around a dysfunctional upbringing and straining as they are harnessed to their past? They drag into each new year the same shame, regret, rejection, sadness, and even anger. Only God can really straighten our lives when we come clean, finally cut the cords, and let go of a shameful past. God can take our past trauma, hurts, shame, and disgrace and weave it into his plan.

4. The fourth bunch shows *how we rationalize our sin.*

Woe to those who call evil good and good evil, who put darkness for light and light for darkness, who put bitter for sweet and sweet for bitter (Isaiah 5:20).

Rationalization is a state of dysfunction where we are messed up in a very bad way but continue to convince ourselves we are fine. Husbands may be unfaithful to their wives but are successfully lying about it. Wives may be spending money and keeping it secret from their husbands. When we rationalize, we know deep down that what we are doing is wrong and it is hurting us and our families, but we tell ourselves everything is fine.

5. The fifth bunch unveils our self-portrait. *We have way too much pride.*

Woe to those who are wise in their own eyes and clever in their own sight (Isaiah 5:21).

The Christian father and mother have the task of learning to depend on God for their strength. Not only is this completely necessary for our success, but it also is how we teach our children. We want them to learn to be God-dependent and not arrogant. This self-confidence that Isaiah is referring to is a refusal to seek God's help. The job of parenting is too big for any of us alone. We need God's help, and he wants to help us.

6. The sixth bunch shows how *the inside affects the outside.*

Woe to those who acquit the guilty for a bribe, but deny justice to the innocent (Isaiah 5:22-23).

The word *woe* means the opposite of blessed. These people are really in a perilous situation, but they don't know it. All the above sour grapes describe the inner condition of his people. The inside affects the outside.

Learning To Be Honest

Authenticity is the one commodity that holds our families together. Without being strong on the inside, we will come apart at the seams when tough times come. For some people, being honest is something that needs to be learned. For example, their pattern of lying may have started very early in their lives, and they find they can't stop it. Some people lie with the primary intention of deception so they can manipulate people. Others lie to avoid conflict; this is the kind of lying that often happens in families, undermining marriages and setting bad examples for children.

One of the best ways to overcome the problem of lying is to be pro-active against it. If you recognize that you have lied to your spouse, then tell them you lied. It greatly helps if the spouse is cooperative and says, "Thank you, and I appreciate your effort to be honest." This kind of action is setting a new pattern that will overcome the old negative one. Without realizing it, spouses set each other up to lie just as parents do with children. If you are a reactive parent and are chomping at the bit to catch your child in a lie, then you are part of the problem.

Children need to learn how to be honest and always tell the truth, and they will do that by seeing us overcome our own problem of lying. Lying is a big problem, and it will only be overcome with intentional effort and help from God. We first have to admit we have a problem before we can work on it.

Learning To Deal With Anger

As a counselor I deal with people on a regular basis who have trouble controlling their anger. I hear all kinds of reasons why they are angry, with the majority of people blaming someone else for their problem. Most of the time people are angry because they are self-centered and haven't learned to delay gratification. Who hasn't seen a two-year-old get angry and begin sulking because he doesn't get his way? When you see an adult with an explosive anger problem, you are looking at an adult with a two-year-old capacity for self-control.

Most of the time people use their anger to control other people. Anger is an effective tool, albeit dysfunctional. It works as long as the other person is willing to respond to the anger. Solomon said, "A hot-tempered man must pay the penalty; if you rescue him, you will have to do it again" (Prov. 19:19). Every time we respond by doing or not doing what some angry person wants from us, we are enabling their anger problem. We are coming to their rescue each time, the same way we do for a small child.

When a person is angry at someone for not responding the way they want them to, they are showing they have no self-control. That's why we often refer to angry people as people who "lose it." The person who is angry is the person with the problem. The challenge comes when you choose to allow the anger to stay in the other person and not allow it to make you angry. As long as we allow the other person's anger to control us, we will remain in bondage to them.

Anger is so often a cue for us to do something. We feel the need to get the angry person's approval or to defend ourselves with responding anger. However, neither of these approaches will help. When we respond appropriately by speaking the truth in love and with the right attitude, we are obligating the other person to choose how they will respond to us.[6]

Sometimes that means we will say something like, "I'm not going to allow you to yell at me. When you calm down and want to talk, I will listen." Such a response oftentimes helps the angry person learn self-control. They will at least learn that their angry rages won't work anymore, and they will need to choose another method of communication. Most importantly, they will learn you cannot be controlled, as you demonstrate you don't have to respond to anger with anger.

There are always consequences to these kinds of choices. Perhaps the person decides not to talk to you at all or to cut you off. You risk those consequences if you want freedom from another person's dysfunctional anger. You will find great freedom in learning self-control.

15

Growing Future Fathers and Mothers

Children clearly learn what they live. Children will live out in childhood, adolescence, and adulthood what they see lived in the home. No child is born with prejudice toward another child, but it does not take long for those attitudes to foment if the parents display them. When we see an adult with an entitlement attitude or a chip on their shoulder, we can most likely understand that it started in their family of origin.

Children need clear boundaries that they understand. They need models that show them how to live within those boundaries. They need their parents to make sense of the world for them. The best protection from a harsh world we can give our children is to help them understand who they are and how to live in this world. Those parents who realize that parenting is too big a job to manage on their own seek wisdom from God. The Bible is full of responsive parenting principles.

Why is it so important to have a good marriage in order to be a good parent? Because you are influencing your children by your marriage. Why is it so important to be honest and authentic with your spouse and children? Because this is the only way to produce that same authenticity in them. Why is it so important to exercise self-control in your interaction with your family? Because you are teaching your children how to interact with others. Why is it so important to have a clear and understandable faith? Because it is the only kind your children will readily accept from you as their own.

In my counseling with parents, I stress to them that children are put at risk when they hear their mother and father complain about each other. It puts children in a bind and places a burden on them they were never meant to carry. No child should ever hear their mother or father criticize the other, no matter how bad things are. Even if they are divorced, children need their parents to respect each other. Responsive parenting has the best interests of the child at heart. This kind of parenting is for the child and for their future. How many parents, in a low moment, have dumped their resentment for their spouse onto their child only later to regret it? The child will most likely continue to carry the burden that was given them.

The same can be said for criticizing other people in the presence of your children. In doing so, you place your prejudice and bias on them. When we look around and see extremely bigoted or ignorant people, we wonder how they got to that place. Bigotry probably happened in the home in which they grew up. It was what was modeled for them in their impressionable years. How we as parents interact with each other is the pattern our children will tend to follow when they become adults. That is a sobering thought!

Children learn how to control their emotions from us, the parents. We can see their progress as they relate to their peers. From very early, we can see how they learn to share and communicate with respect. If we have valued their emotions and are teaching them to value another person's feelings as well, then that is good parenting.[1]

Our children will learn to tolerate negative emotion, such as being patient with another person who is upset or angry, if they have seen us do so. If they have felt our impatience and disregard for their feelings and desires, they will do the same with their peers. If, on the other hand, they have seen patience modeled and respect demonstrated, they will follow that model. If they have seen our determination to be truthful and honest time and time again, then they will follow that pattern. They will follow us in our thought pattern, in our management of our emotions, and in our behavior.

The Way Parents Treat Teenagers

Parents treat teenagers in three dominate ways. The first is that they treat them as if they are completely grown and capable of making all their own decisions. The parents take a back seat position and allow the teenagers to make major decisions for their own lives with little input from them. The second way is that the parents continue to treat the teenagers as if they are still children, which causes considerable resentment.

The third way is the responsive one of interacting with teenagers. This approach gives more freedom as the teenager demonstrates more responsibility. It is a relational approach where you can be very involved but in a respectful way in their lives. This way of relating to teenagers is entirely possible if you have been involved in your child's life for the previous twelve years.

In the teen years, important decisions are being made that will affect the rest of their lives, so it is irresponsible to withdraw your parental involvement. Unfortunately, that often happens because the relationship has already broken down. When parents and teenagers are still very relationally connected, on the other hand, this is an exciting time because you can help them explore their autonomy in a responsible way.

At this point you can help them get a job, learn to be a productive employee, and manage their money. As they formulate their own philosophical views and opinions about life and people, you can have meaningful discussions with them. You help them plan their future by exploring their educational and career goals with them. You discuss their questions about life, faith, and family by not dodging any of them, but by helping them find answers. You are there when they make wrong decisions to help them learn from their mistakes. This kind of relationship keeps them moving in a productive direction and keeps you connected to them.

As we watch this growing autonomy, we have to resist the idea of protecting our teens from making any mistakes. Mistakes are a part of life and will often provide our teens with the right curriculum they need to learn from them. We have to help them, but that doesn't mean building a bubble around them so nothing painful ever comes their way.

Finding Their Own Identity

Several years ago my father accompanied me on a trip to speak at a youth camp in Salta, one of the northern provinces of Argentina. We rode a bus to get there with all the luggage stacked on top of the bus. When we arrived in Salta several hours later, my dad's suitcase was not there. He had to live out of my suitcase for the entire camp. It was uncomfortable because he had to wear clothes that didn't fit him properly.

After we returned home, an interesting thing happened later that week in the city of Tucuman where we lived. Our neighbour, Mussy, after hearing of our plight with the missing suitcase, noticed in the newspaper that the police had published a "found" notice of a suitcase belonging to Mr. G. N. Brooks. We immediately went to the police and surprisingly were able to reclaim the lost suitcase. Even though it had fallen off the bus over 200 miles away, someone had dropped it off in our city.

It's ironic in life how many people have misplaced or lost their God-given suitcase and are living life out of someone else's suitcase. They are impressed with someone else's talent or skill or beauty, and they are trying to be that somebody else. Sometimes we allow other people to give us their suitcase, such as a parent or grandparent. How much better to find our own suitcase of skills, talents, and personality, and use what God has given us for his glory! Only when we are who we were meant to be will we be content.

Helping your child find his own suitcase is a challenging but exciting task. At first he will live out of yours, but as time progresses you will notice his distinct differences and come to appreciate them all. Encourage those pursuits that interest your child. They won't all be worthwhile, but eventually you will find the right one, and what a delight it will be to see your child dressed in their own personality, skills, talents, and occupation.

16

❧

Passing the Torch of Faith

Throughout this book I have been talking about how to help your child connect the dots so they will be prepared for adult life. We have talked about: *forgiveness,* a*ccessibility, making meaning out of chaos, connection, acceptance, resolution, turning negative emotion into positive emotion, modeling, self-control, authenticity,* and *resiliency.* However, the list would not be complete without talking about *faith.* Faith is the essential component that children need to finish the picture. Specifically, they need to see your faith modeled in front of them. They need to see and experience a faith that makes sense—a faith that works.

Sometimes life can be so humdrum and repetitious that we fail to see the big picture of what it means. Responsible parents learn how to be big picture parents. Georges Seurat was a big picture person. He introduced a technique known as pointillism, which is a portrait painted from thousands of tiny dots. From up close it just looks like so many dots, but as you back away, the picture begins to emerge. The introduction of faith to your child will seem like thousands of dots at first until you help them find the big picture.[1]

We need to realize that our children see our faith as a lot of details that they don't yet understand. That is why it is so important to help them get the big picture of what God is doing in this world and in our lives. The Bible is filled with all kinds of literature, history, poetry, law, gospels, and prophetic books, to mention a few. Children need help to understand how they all fit together. One of the most intriguing ways to make sense of your faith for your children is to help them see how Christianity works.

Christianity offers the best explanation for life's most complex questions such as, "How did I get here?" "What is my purpose in life?" Where am I going?" and "How did the world get to be such a mess?" The sooner we help our children begin to answer these questions through faith, the more meaningful life will be for them. Our faith not only helps us answer these questions, it also shows us how to treat each other and how to live in this world.

We have so many distractions in life that make it hard for us to see God's big picture for our lives. We struggle with our health, our money, our interpersonal relationships, and so many other things—and they all just look like dots. However, as we learn to focus on God's big picture, we see how to connect them all and understand what really matters in life. C.S. Lewis wrote in *Mere Christianity* that we were created by God and for God:

> God made us: invented us as a man invents an engine. A car is made to run on gasoline, and it would not run properly on anything else. Now God designed the human machine to run on Himself. He Himself is the fuel our spirits were designed to burn, or the food our spirits were designed to feed on. There is no other. That is why it is just no good asking God to make us happy in our own way without bothering about religion. God cannot give us a happiness and peace apart from Himself, because it is not there. There is no such thing.[2]

As Lewis so eloquently states, we will never find our purpose without finding our place in God's universe and allowing him first place in our lives. In doing this and teaching this to our children, we will be preparing them to live and to die. The Christian faith, when understood, not only gives us purpose for living, but also courage to face impossible situations. Dietrich Bonhoeffer says that when faith is alive, it transforms life and death for us.

Prepared To Live and Die

Dietrich Bonhoeffer, the German pastor who stood up to Nazism, wrote about death shortly before he was executed by Hitler. As he painted a big picture with his words, it's clear that God had helped him focus on what really mattered in this life. Life is meaningful when you know the One who created you and made a purpose for your life. Likewise, death is only dreadful for those who have no hope beyond death. Bonhoeffer wrote, "Death is hell and night and cold, if it is not transformed by our faith. But that is just what is so marvelous, that we can transform death."[3]

Bonhoeffer's words are so insightful because he says faith can transform death so that we do not have to dread it. Faith actually transforms life and death for those who possess genuine faith and really know Jesus Christ as Lord and Savior.

Learning that Jesus can help us both in our daily situations and in our catastrophes can make the difference between living right and living wrong. Jesus' own disciples had to learn this. Once at the end of a long day, Jesus told his disciples, "Let us go over to the other side of the lake" (Luke 8:22). Jesus chose to rest in the boat as the disciples made their way across the lake. Then suddenly, the normally tranquil lake became the scene of a massive storm. The winds caused huge waves that hurled the boat up and down, leaving the disciples panic stricken. The disciples reacted with fear, as most of us do when we experience danger or troubling situations.

Once in Argentina, a friend and I were fishing with our sons on the Parana River. We fished for Dorado and Surubi and caught some magnificent ones. Abruptly, however, the wind came up, and the waves started to rock the boat. We decided it was time to head to shore when suddenly the motor quit, causing us some panic. The swift current carried us quickly downstream, and we were still over a half mile from shore. We hoped we might be seen by a coast guard station up ahead, but if they didn't see us, we would be in for a long ride on a very rough river. I took off my vest and started waving it back and forth, and fortunately a coast guard boat showed up and towed us to shore. We were immensely thankful to be on land after facing such a scary moment on the water. My experience helps me appreciate the disciples' fears.

Without life's difficulties, however, we would never grow spiritually, and our walk with God would be so shallow. The tests we endure reveal our character and the reality of our faith.

Jesus was sleeping in the stern of the boat in the middle of the storm. While the boat was taking a beating and the disciples were plunged into dark despair, Jesus was resting from his extreme weariness. The storm brought fear to the disciples, so they went and woke him, saying, "Master, Master, we're going to drown!" (Luke 8:24). The disciples were paralyzed with fear that they were going to die.

After Jesus rebuked the wind and the raging waters, the storm subsided, and all was calm (Luke 8:24). Nothing could have compared to this experience. Jesus asked his disciples,

"Where is your faith?" Their faith had been overcome by their fear, but now they could see what they couldn't see a few moments before: "Who is this? He commands even the winds and the water, and they obey him" (Luke 8:25). Jesus can calm any storm because he is Lord of creation.

Sometimes the tests are from storms outside of our power, but other times they come from inside of us. Discouragement, for example, is a real obstacle to our progress in life. Just when we think things are beginning to go in our direction, something happens, and we suffer a setback. We all know what discouragement feels like because we all have dealt with it.

It is important to remember that Jesus lived like us in a human body with the full gamut of human emotions, and though he did not sin, he knows our weaknesses. Jesus trusted God with the future, with his work, and with the problems he encountered. He never abandoned his faith, nor did he turn away in cynical unbelief, though he was tempted to do so. He deliberately chose to trust God with each setback. What an example for all of us.

Let's apply these principles to life. For example, it's clear that arguing and fighting in front of your children is very harmful to them. But if you have a habit of arguing frequently, how do you just stop overnight? The answer is you don't. First of all, begin to pray about this and ask for God's help. Second, see a counselor who will work with you to develop and use some practical strategies. The following are some of the strategies I use when working with couples who argue in front of their children:

Levels of Conflict: It is helpful to understand the three levels of conflict: The first level is discussion, which is healthy. It is where husband and wife state their opinions and the other listens and learns. The next level is arguing, which is an "I'm right; you're wrong" mentality. That quickly escalates into the third level which is fighting, where each is trying to hurt the other with their words and actions.

The "Never" List: This is a list that each partner makes of hurtful words they have frequently used in the past but now promise to never say to the other when they get angry. If they mess up, which they probably will, they will apologize and return to keeping the promise.

The Discussion Method: The discussion method is best learned with the help of a counselor. One states their complaint, and the other listens and waits a few moments to respond. Self-reflection is always helpful in order to see what they could not see about their own attitudes and behavior when they are angry.

Calling a Truce: When a couple realizes they are arguing and quickly moving toward a devastating fight, it's time to call a truce. Either partner can do it by simply stating the obvious fact that they are not making progress through their discussion, and so they should wait and bring this up later. When it is brought up later and discussed, each one can talk about their own shortfalls.

When a couple finds themselves in an argument in front of their children, they need the Lord to calm the storm. In this scenario, their emotions are out of control, and the kids will be confused and frightened. In the middle of the moment, the Lord will respond to your request for help and give you the courage and strength to call a truce and apologize to the family for any inappropriate remarks or actions. That is what God can do, and it will save your children from future anxiety and dysfunction in their own adult life.

Calling a Family Meeting: In the middle of a truce is the time to call your first family meeting and freely admit to the whole family that the two of you are struggling. Apologize and tell everyone how much you love each other and let the family know what you are working toward. The kids will support you and help you when they sense your sincerity. Remember that deception cancels out authenticity, but truthfulness reinforces it. You need courage to do something like that. That is what I call a moment where God calms the storm and brings peace to troubled hearts.

Sharing My Faith With My Grandchildren

Being a grandpa is great! What can I say but that I think this is about the best job I have ever had. I love being a dad, and I love being a grandpa. At the moment I have seven, little, precious lives that call me by that name. I feel such pride when I hear their voices call me as if I were being given an honored status. I get hugs, kisses, and so much attention. They ask me questions, and they expect me to know all the answers. I tell them about things they are learning about for the very first time. Believe me, I am influencing their little lives, as they are mine. They tell me stories and startle me with little phrases that leave me wondering where that came from.

How privileged I am to be married to the same woman for 45 years and have kids that love and respect me and grandkids that shower me with love and affection. I have seen every kind of family problem in my years of working with families, and I know what I have. I have seen families torn apart by divorce, shattered by an abandoned father, or devastated by a mother who left them for another man. I have felt the pain of a family traumatized by the hopelessness of addiction. I have seen families confused by unfaithfulness, embittered by betrayal, and left estranged by abuse and shame, and my heart goes out to all of them.

I know that I am blessed and that God has done this for me. My wife and I have given our family an example of faithfulness, but we know that God has enabled us to do this despite our many flaws. I have what money can't buy—an intimate relationship with my wife and children, which has given me this unique relationship with these little people who call me grandpa.

Society and culture tell me that my worth is seen in the external props, but I know better. Personally, I couldn't care less what society thinks, but I do care what God thinks and what my family thinks. I know my worth and purpose come from deep within and from my relationship with my Creator.

By pursuing what is inherently right—the values God has given you in his Word—you will be on the right parenting road. You will find yourself surrounded by wealth, and on top of the list will be your family.

Appendix

Important Biblical Concepts
for Responsive Parenting

Forgiveness is the key to enjoying life. Through it we renew and invigorate our relationships. It is God's gift to us to manage and repair difficult mistakes in our lives. It is more of a process than it is an act. If we learn to appreciate forgiveness, it will be like a giant shredder that eliminates the junk accumulating in our lives.

Self-control is the ability to control your emotions, especially those powerful ones like anger, frustration, rejection, and discouragement. This incredibly important ability has to be learned, and the classes should start with toddlers. Self-control is the foundation for all the other disciplines of life. We can learn that good, healthy thoughts can reign in those unhealthy emotions, giving us control of our lives. If our parents model this behavior, it will be much easier; if they don't, it will be so much more difficult to acquire this essential ability.

Respect is the esteem for the inherent worth of a person. Respect is the proper way to treat people, and it doesn't come naturally. In fact disrespect seems to be more natural. We have to be taught how to be respectful to others—beginning with our parents and those in authority.

Responsibility is a crucial concept essential for a child to learn if they hope to arrive at adulthood with a good foundation. The earlier we learn responsibility, the earlier we start being responsible for our own actions. It is responsible to forgive, to share, to help, to not blame, to correct, to improve, and to make right what is wrong in our actions. We are people who make mistakes, but we have to learn to take responsibility for them.

Accountability is the concept that teaches us that we are answerable to someone—first to God and then to our parents and those who are in authority. Learning to be accountable is a quality that will help a child be a better spouse, a better parent, a better employee, and a better friend. We all need accountability because it helps hold us in check. Without it, we would be like the water in a river without levees.

Humility means that a person has a modest estimate of his own importance compared to other people. Pride, on the other hand, means a person has an inordinate opinion of his own importance. Humility is authenticity on display in a person who is easy to talk to and interesting to listen to. Humility feels no compulsion to impress anyone; and yet, wherever the humble person goes, he leaves a lasting impression.

Kindness is the quality of being considerate or showing a kind act to another person. As God shows us kindness, we learn to pass that kindness along to others with our words, facial expressions, body language, actions, and our whole disposition. It's kindness that considers another's needs and tries to meet them.

Generosity is sharing in an unselfish manner. It is a willingness to give or share what we possess with others and especially with those in need. Generosity creates magnanimous hearts, which includes not being easily offended.

Industry is diligence in a pursuit or task. It is so meaningful to find work for your children and to help them learn to pursue it and do their best. It helps them to appreciate work and become reliable while learning the value of hard-earned money.

Faith is a visible demonstration of our relationship with God. Nothing is as powerful and transformative to a child as to see their parents live out their faith in a consistent manner. If God is a vital part of their lives, then family life will be the foremost arena where that faith is at work.

The success of marriages and of entire families hinge on these principles. When a family will acknowledge that things are not good and they need help, they are candidates for transformation that comes through these effective principles.

The Results of Faithfully Teaching Biblical Concepts

Accessibility is that closeness that allows us to have a connection with our parents while we are growing up. If we find it, we will more than likely be connected to those people closest to us as an adult. Examining whether or not you have this with your children is imperative, and it's never too late to acquire it.

Clarity means making meaning out of chaos, and that is what God does for us when we allow his grace to work in our hearts. This concept has two parts: first is our part, which is learning to be flexible and not rigid when things don't go the way we expect. Secondly, it is what God does behind the scenes to make meaning out of confusion for us. This concept, when applied, transforms chaos into purpose and hurts into life lessons.

Balance is dealing with both negative and positive emotion in what we deal with every day. Learning to turn negative emotions into positive ones is what we call successful living. The difference between positive and negative emotion is often simply a choice. It begins with setting healthy boundaries and guidelines for communication and then learning to treat each other with more respect.

Connection is a powerful word used repeatedly to describe the relationship between the mother and father and between each parent and child. It is an emotional link that generates healthy emotions and makes relationships enjoyable and meaningful.

Acceptance is how we win the battle over shame; this has to do with our acceptance of our children and their understanding of God's acceptance of them. We have all experienced shame, but we all haven't recovered from it; it's the part we still carry around that gives us problems. Acceptance is God's way of freeing us from the chains of shame.

Authenticity is the quality of character that says you are real. The person who possesses this has to work at keeping it because every mistake is an occasion to lose it or strengthen it depending on how we handle it.

Resolution is what we do with conflict, and it makes all the difference in the world. Conflict is inevitable, but our willingness to work it out can change how our children see the world. Many families are stuck in a repetitive cycle of conflict and have no idea how to stop it. This book points those families in the direction of working on resolution and exchanging deadly patterns for healthy ones.

Modeling is a living example of a parent who displays these qualities in front of his family. Children learn from watching a model and taking on those values and qualities as their own. Modeling personifies for the child what it means to be a husband, wife, mother, or father.

Resiliency is the ability to come back and not allow disappointment and discouragement to push you down. Children who are loved and accepted will demonstrate this quality. They will show a resilient spirit in life that will enable them to be overcomers.

Any good financial advisor would tell you the best way to build wealth is to build it slowly and consistently. Likewise, the best way to build strong, healthy families is to invest slowly and deliberately over the years. Invest in your family by living out these principles, and you will reap the rewards of these outcomes.

Endnotes

Chapter One

1 Jennifer C. Ablow, Jeffrey Measelle, Philip A. Cowan, and Carolyn P. Cowan, "Linking Marital Conflict and Children's Adjustment: The Role of Young Children's Perceptions," *Journal of Family Psychology,* 23, no. 4 (2009): 485-499. doi:10.1037/a0015894

2 Matthew D. Bramlett and William D. Mosher, "Cohabitation, Marriage, Divorce, and Remarriage in the United States," *Vital & Health Statistics,* 23, no. 22 (2002): 1-103.

3 Brene Brown, *Daring Greatly: How the Courage to Be Vulnerable Transforms the Way We Live, Love, Parent, and Lead* (Penguin Group US, 2012), 69. Kindle Edition.

4 Alithe Van den Akker, Maja Dkovic, Rebecca Shiner, Jessica Asscher, and Peter Prinzie, "Personality Types in Childhood: Relations to Latent Trajectory Classes of Problem Behavior and Overreactive Parenting Across the Transition into Adolescence," *Journal of Personality and Social Psychology,* 104, no. 4 (2013): 750-764. doi:10.1037/a0031184

Chapter Two

1 Meghan B. Serimgeour, Alysia Y. Blandon, Cynthia A. Stifter, and Kristin A. Buss, "Cooperative Coparenting Moderates the Association Between Parenting Practices and Children's Prosocial Behavior," *Journal of Family Psychology,* 27, no. 3 (2013): 506-511. doi:10.1037/a0032893

2 Robert J. Coplan, Linda Rose-Kransor, Murray Weeks, Adam Kingsbury, Mila Kingsbury, and Amanda Bullock, "Alone Is a Crowd: Social Motivations, Social Withdrawal, and Socioemotional Functioning in Later Childhood," *Developmental Psychology,* 49, no. 5 (2013): 861-875.

3 Sara A. Heimpel, Joanne V. Wood, Margaret A. Marshall, and Jonathan D. Brown, "Do People with Low Self-Esteem Really Want to Feel Better? Self-Esteem Differences in Motivation to Repair Negative Moods." *Journal of Personality and Social Psychology,* 82, no. 1 (2002): 128-147. doi:10.1037//0022-351482.1.128

4 Darby E. Saxbe, Michelle R. Ramos, Adele C. Timmons, Aubrey R. Rodriguez, and Gayla Margolin, "A Path Modeling Approach to Understanding Family Conflict: Reciprocal Patterns of Parent Coercion and Adolescent Avoidance," *Journal of Family Psychology,* 28, no. 3 (2014): 415-420. doi:10.1037/a0036817

Chapter Three

1 Megan Ubinger, Paul J. Handal, and Carrie E. Massura, "Adolescent Adjustment: The Hazards of Conflict Avoidance and the Benefits of

Conflict Resolution," *Psychology,* 4, no. 1 (2013): 50-58.
doi:10.4236/psych.2013.41007

2 E. Mark Cummings and Julie N. Schatz, "Family Conflict, Emotional
Security, and Child Development: Translating Research Findings into a
Prevention Program for Community Families," *Clinical Child Family
Psychology Review,* 15 (2012): 14-17. doi:10.1007/s10567-012-0112-0

3 Brian R.W. Baucom, Darby Saxbe, Michelle C. Ramos, Lauren A.
Spies Shapiro, Esti Iturralde, Sarah Duman, and Gayla Margolin,
"Correlates and Characteristics of Adolescent's Encoded Emotional
Arousal During Family Conflict," *Emotion,* 12, no. 6 (2012): 1281-1291.
doi:10.1037/a0028872

4 Jennifer A. Bailey, Karl G. Hill, Katarina Guttmannova, Sabrina
Oesterle, J. David Hawkins, Richard F. Catalano, and Robert J.
McMahon, "The Association Between Parent Early Adult Drug Use
Disorder and Later Observed Parenting Practices and Child Behavior
Problems: Testing Alternate Models," *Developmental Psychology,* 49, no.
5 (2013): 887-899. doi:10.1037/a0029235

5 Survey conducted by the author of four different adult groups in 2014.

6 Meghan B. Serimgeour, Alysia Y. Blandon, Cynthia A. Stifter, and
Kristin A. Buss, "Cooperative Coparenting Moderates the Association
Between Parenting Practices and Children's Prosocial Behavior," *Journal
of Family Psychology,* 27, no. 3 (2013): 506-511. doi:10.1037/a0032893

Chapter Four

1 Diane L. Putnick, Marc H. Bornstein, Charlene Hendricks, Kathleen M.
Painter, Joan T. D. Suwalsky, and W. Andrew Collins, "Parenting Stress,
Perceived Parenting Behaviors, and Adolescent Self-Concept in European
American Families," *Journal of Family Psychology,* 22, no. 5 (2008):
752-762. doi:10.1037/a0013177

2 Mih Viorel, "Role of Parental Support for Learning, Autonomous/
Control Motivation, and Forms of Self-Regulation on Academic
Attainment in High School Students: A Path Analysis. Cognition, Brain,
Behavior," *An Interdisciplinary Journal,* 18, no. 1 (2013): 35-59.

3 Doret J. De Ruyter and Anders Schinkel, "On the Relations Between
Parents' Ideals and Children's Autonomy," *Educational Theory,* 63, no. 4
(2013): 369-388.

4 Walter Mischel and Ebbe B. Ebbesen, "Attention in Delay of
Gratification," *Journal of Personality and Social Psychology,* 16, no. 2
(October 1970): 329–337. doi:10.1037/h0029815

5 Bettina F. Piko and Mate A. Balazs, "Control or Involvement?

Relationship Between Authoritative Parenting Style and Adolescent Depressive Symptomatology," *European Child Adolescent Psychiatry,* 21 (2012): 149-155. doi:10.1007/s00787-012-0246-0

6 Veronika Huta, "Linking People's Pursuit of Eudaimonia and Hedonia with Characteristics of Their Parents: Parenting Styles, Verbally Endorsed Values, and Role Modeling," *Springer Science & Business Media,* 13 (2012): 47-61. doi:10.1007/s10902-011-9249-7

7 Ming-Te Wang, Thomas J. Dishion, Elizabeth A. Stormshak, and John B. Willett, "Trajectories of Family Management Practices and Early Adolescent Behavioral Outcomes," *Developmental Psychology,* 47, no. 5 (2011): 1324-1341. doi:10.1037/a0024026

Chapter Five
1 Randy Carlson, as quoted by Charles Swindoll, "Uplifting Words for Strung Out Dads," CDR-SCC525 June 2007.

2 Scott R. Braithwaite, Edward A. Selby, and Frank D. Fincham, "Forgiveness and Relationship Satisfaction: Mediating Mechanisms," *Journal of Family Psychology,* 25, no. 4 (2011): 551-559. doi:10.1037/a0024526

3 Kristina Coop Gordon, Farrah M. Hughes, Nathan D. Tomcik, Lee J. Dixon, and Samantha C. Litzinger, "Widening Spheres of Impact: The Role of Forgiveness in Marital and Family Functioning," *Journal of Family Psychology,* 23, no. 1 (2009): 1-13. doi:10.1037/a0014354

4 Dick Keyes, *Beyond Identity* (Great Britain: Paternoster Press, 1998), 211.

5 Viktor Frankl, *Man's Search for Meaning* (Boston: Beacon Press, 2006), XIII.

6 Sam A. Hardy, Jennifer A. White, Zhiyong Zhang, and Joshua Ruchty, "Parenting and the Socialization of Religiousness and Spirituality," *Psychology of Religion and Spirituality,* 3, no. 3 (2011): 217-230. doi:10.1037/a0021600

Chapter Six
1 Per Ola d'Aulaire and Emily d'Aulaire, as quoted by James Dobson, "Now What Are They Doing at That Crazy St. John the Divine?" *Smithsonian Magazine,* 23, no. 9 (December 1992): 32.

Chapter Seven
1 Maire B. Ford and Nancy L. Collins, "Self-Esteem Moderates Neuroendocrine and Psychological Responses to Interpersonal

Rejection," *Journal of Personality and Social Psychology,* 98, no. 3 (2010): 752-762. doi:10.1037/0017345

2 Stephen W. Porges, "Neuroception: A Subconscious System for Detecting Threats and Safety," *Zero to Three,* 25, no. 5 (2004): 19-24.

3 W. Robert Beavers and Robert B. Hampson, "The Beavers Systems Model of Family Functioning," *Journal of Family Therapy,* 22 (2000): 128-143.

4 Tara Thacher and Dan Bailis, "Selective Defensiveness or Nondefensiveness: How Does Relative Autonomy Relate to Excuse-Making When Goal Pursuits Do Not Succeed?," *Motivation and Emotion,* 36 (2012): 323-337. doi:10.1007//s11031-011-9248-3

5 Andrew Christensen, Brian Doss, and Neil Jacobson, *Reconcilable Differences* (Guilford Publications, 1999), 11-12. Kindle Edition.

6 Fay C. M. Geisler and Hannelore Weber, "Harm That Does Not Hurt: Humour in Coping with Self-Threat," *Motivation and Emotion,* 34 (2010): 446-456. doi:10.1007/s11031-010-9185-6

7 Philip Graham Ryken, *Exodus* (Wheaton, IL: Crossway Books, 2005), 519.

Chapter Eight

1 Maureen Waller, "Cooperation, Conflict, or Disengagement? Coparenting Styles and Father Involvement in Fragile Families," *Family Process,* 51, no. 3 (2012): 325-342.

2 Anthony Biglan, Brian R. Flay, Dennis D. Embry, and Irwin N. Sandler, "The Critical Role of Nurturing Environments for Promoting Human Well-Being," *American Psychologists,* 67, no. 4 (2012): 257-271. doi:101037/a0026796

3 Carolyn Ha, Carla Sharp, and Ian Goodyer, "The Role of Child and Parental Mentalizing for the Development of Conduct Problems over Time," *European Child Adolescent Psychiatry,* 20 (2011): 291-300. doi:10.1007/s00787-011-0174-4

4 Anne Martin, Rebecca M. Ryan, and Jeanne Brooks-Gunn, "When Father's Supportiveness Matters Most: Maternal and Paternal Parenting and Children's School Readiness," *Journal of Family Psychology,* 24, no. 2 (2010): 145-155. doi:10.1037/a0018073

5 Emily Bariola, Eleonora Gullone, and Elizabeth Hughes, "Child and Adolescent Emotion Regulation: The Role of Parental Emotion Regulation and Expression," *Clinical Child Family Psychology,* 14 (2011): 198-212. doi:10.1007/s10567-011-0092-5

6 Lewis Smedes, "The Power of Promises." In Thomas G. Long and Cornelius Plantinga, Jr (Eds.), *A Chorus of Witnesses* (Grand Rapids, MI: Erdmans, 1994).

7 E. Mark Cummings and Julie N. Schatz, "Family Conflict, Emotional Security, and Child Development: Translating Research Findings into a Prevention Program for Community Families," *Clinical Child Family Psychology Review,* 15 (2012): 14-17. doi:10.1007/s10567-012-0112-0

8 Bo-Ram Kim and Douglas M. Teti, "Maternal Emotional Availability During Infant Bedtime: An Ecological Framework," *Journal of Family Psychology,* 28, no. 1 (2014): 1-11. doi:10.1037/a0035157

9 Amy Strage and Tamara Swanson Brandt, "Authoritative Parenting and College Students' Academic Adjustment and Success," *Journal of Educational Psychology,* 91, no. 1 (1999): 146-156.

10 P. Tyler Roskos, Paul J. Handal, and Megan E. Ubinger, "Family Conflict Resolution: Its Measurement and Relationship with Family Conflict and Psychological Adjustment," *Psychology,* 1, no. 5 (2010): 370-376. doi:104236/psych.2010.15046

11 Annemiek Karreman, Cathy Van Tuijl, Marcel A. G. Van Aken, and Maja Dekovic "Parenting, Coparenting, and Effortful Control in Preschoolers," *Journal of Family Psychology,* 22, no. 1 (2008): 30-40. doi:10.1037/0893-3200.22.1.30

12 Patrick J. Sweeney and Louis W. Fry, "Character Development Through Spiritual Leadership," *Consulting Psychology Journal: Practice and Research,* 64, no. 2 (2012): 89-107. doi:10.1037/a0028966

13 Sam A. Hardy, Jennifer A. White, Zhiyong Zhang, and Joshua Ruchty, "Parenting and the Socialization of Religiousness and Spirituality," *Psychology of Religion and Spirituality,* 3, no. 3 (2011): 217-230. doi:10.1037/a0021600

Chapter Nine
1 Jean Edward Smith, *Grant* (Simon & Schuster, 2001), 363-373. Kindle Edition.

2 June P. Tangney and Ronda L. Dearing, *Shame and Guilt* (New York, NY: Guilford Press, 2002), 171.

3 Ibid, p. 18.

4 Ibid, p. 91-92.

5 Stephanie Pappas Interviews Nathan Fox. See https://www.live-science.com/21778-early-neglect-alters-kids-brains.html

6 Dave Ziegler, *Traumatic Experience and the Brain: A Handbook for*

Understanding and Treating Those Traumatized as Children (Acacia Publishing, Inc., 2011), 671-673. Kindle Edition.

7 See https://www.livescience.com/21778-early-neglect-alters-kids-brains.html.

8 Nathan Fox, Heather A. Henderson, Kenneth H. Rubin, Susan D. Calkins, and Louis A. Schmidt, "Continuity and Discontinuity of Behavioral Inhibition and Exuberance: Psychophysiological and Behavioral Influence across the First Four Years of Life," *Child Development,* 72, no.1 (2001): 1-21.

9 See http://www.npr.org/sections/health-shots/2014/02/20/280237833/orphans-lonely-beginnings-reveal-how-parents-shape-a-childs-brain.html.

10 Gregory A. Freeman, *The Forgotten 500: The Untold Story of the Men Who Risked All for the Greatest Rescue Mission of World War II* (Penguin Publishing Group US, 2008), 3809-3810. Kindle Edition.

11 Brene Brown, *Daring Greatly: How the Courage to Be Vulnerable Transforms the Way We Live, Love, Parent, and Lead* (Penguin Group US, 2012), 51-52. Kindle Edition.

Chapter Ten
1 Tom White, *The Voice of the Martyrs* (VOM). September 2008 issue of VOM's monthly newsletter.

2 Lewis Smedes, *Forgive & Forget* (New York: Pocket Books, 1984), 39-40.

3 Henry Cloud, *The Power of the Other: The Startling Effect Other People Have on You, from the Boardroom to the Bedroom and Beyond—and What to Do About It* (New York, NY: HarperCollins, 2016), 226-229. Kindle Edition.

Chapter Eleven
1 C.S. Lewis, *The Great Divorce* (Great Britain: Harper One, 2001), 106-108.

2 Ibid, p. 110-114.

3 Ibid, p. 112-114.

Chapter Twelve
1 Marian Diamond and Janet Hopson, *Magic Trees of the Mind* (New York: Plumb Book, 1998).

2 Elmer Bendiner as told by Charles Swindoll, "Our Favorite Sin," CDR-SCC1001, May 24, 2015.

Chapter Thirteen

1 Aracely Maldonado, *Solo un Peon.*

2 Don Anderson, *Joseph Fruitful in Affliction* (Neptune, New Jersey: Loizeaux Brothers, 1988), 60.

Chapter Fourteen

1 John M. Gottman and Nan Silver, *The Seven Principles for Making Marriage Work* (New York: Three Rivers Press, 1999), 25-33.

2 Lewis Smedes, *Love Within Limits: A Realist's View of 1 Corinthians 13* (Grand Rapids, MI: Eerdmans, 1978), 58.

3 John M. Gottman and Daniel Goleman, *Raising An Emotionally Intelligent Child* (Simon & Schuster, 2011), 184-185. Kindle Edition.

4 Alan Redpath, *The Making of a Man of God* (Grand Rapids, MI: Fleming H. Revell, 1990), 128.

5 Bev Savage, "Free and Focused," *PreachingToday* audio, Issue 281, 2006.

6 Henry Cloud and John Townsend, *Boundaries* (Nashville, TN: Zondervan, 1992), 248-249.

Chapter Fifteen

1 John M. Gottman and Daniel Goleman, *Raising An Emotionally Intelligent Child* (Simon & Schuster, 2011), 180. Kindle Edition.

Chapter Sixteen

1 Philip Graham Ryken, *Exodus* (Wheaton, IL: Crossway Books, 2005), 911.

2 C.S. Lewis, *Mere Christianity* (New York: MacMillian Publishing, 1943), 55.

3 Eric Metaxas, *Bonhoeffer: Pastor, Martyr, Prophet, Spy* (Nashville, TN: Thomas Nelson, 2010), 10448-10454. Kindle Edition.

About the Author

Boyd Brooks has been in ministry for over thirty years both as a missionary to Argentina and as a pastor. He has been married for forty-six years and has three grown children and seven grandchildren. His family has been his greatest priority in life, and so he has made helping families the center of his ministry. He also writes a weekly blog that keeps him thinking and writing.

Boyd has a doctorate in psychology and is a licensed professional counselor in the state of Missouri. From his many years of counseling families, he has a wealth of experience to draw upon. His passion is to help young families by building strong marriages and a good parenting style. He believes that whenever parents adopt a responsible parenting style—from these homes emerge children who are strong emotionally, cognitively, and spiritually.

Connect with the author at:
boydbrooks.com